Lives of the Poets

Samuel Johnson

Table of Contents

Lives of the Poets

Samuel Johnson

INTRODUCTION.

This volume contains a record of twenty lives, of which only one— that of Edward Young—is treated at length. It completes our edition of Johnson's Lives of the Poets, from which a few only of the briefest and least important have been omitted.

The eldest of the Poets here discussed were Samuel Garth, Charles Montague (Lord Halifax), and William King, who were born within the years 1660–63. Next in age were Addison's friend Ambrose Philips, and Nicholas Rowe the dramatist, who was also the first editor of Shakespeare's plays after the four folios had appeared. Ambrose Philips and Rowe were born in 1671 and 1673, and Isaac Watts in 1674. Thomas Parnell, born in 1679, would follow next, nearly of like age with Young, whose birth–year was 1681. Pope's friend John Gay was of Pope's age, born in 1688, two years later than Addison's friend Thomas Tickell, who was born in 1686. Next in the course of years came, in 1692, William Somerville, the author of "The Chace." John Dyer, who wrote "Grongar Hill," and James Thomson, who wrote the "Seasons," were both born in the year 1700. They were two of three poets—Allan Ramsay, the third—who, almost at the same time, wrote verse instinct with a fresh sense of outward Nature which was hardly to be found in other writers of that day. David Mallet, Thomson's college–friend and friend of after–years—who shares with Thomson the curiosity of critics who would decide which of them wrote "Rule Britannia"—was of Thomson's age.

The other writers of whose lives Johnson here gives his note were men born in the beginning of the eighteenth century: Gilbert West, the translator of Pindar, in 1706; George Lyttelton, in 1709. William Shenstone, whose sense of Nature, although true, was mixed with the conventions of his time, and who once asked a noble friend to open a waterfall in the garden upon which the poet spent his little patrimony, was born in 1714; Thomas Gray, in 1716; William Collins, in 1720; and Mark Akenside, in 1721. In Collins, while he lived with loss of reason, Johnson, who had fears for himself, took pathetic interest. Akenside could not interest him much. Akenside made his mark when young with "The Pleasures of Imagination," a good poem, according to the fashion of the time, when read with due consideration as a young man's first venture for fame. He spent much of the rest of his life in overloading it with valueless additions. The writer who begins well should let well alone, and, instead of tinkering at bygone work, follow the course of his own ripening thought. He should seek new ways of doing worthy service in the years of labour left to him.

H. M.

KING.

William King was born in London in 1663; the son of Ezekiel King, a gentleman. He was allied to the family of Clarendon.

From Westminster School, where he was a scholar on the foundation under the care of Dr. Busby, he was at eighteen elected to Christ Church in 1681; where he is said to have prosecuted his studies with so much intenseness and activity, that before he was eight years' standing he had read over, and made remarks upon, twenty–two thousand odd hundred books and manuscripts. The books were certainly not very long, the manuscripts not very difficult, nor the remarks very large; for the calculator will find that he despatched seven a day for every day of his eight years; with a remnant that more than satisfies most other students. He took his degree in the most expensive manner, as a GRAND COMPOUNDER; whence it is inferred that he inherited a considerable fortune.

In 1688, the same year in which he was made Master of Arts, he published a confutation of Varillas's account of Wickliffe; and, engaging in the study of the civil law, became Doctor in 1692, and was admitted advocate at Doctors' Commons.

He had already made some translations from the French, and written some humorous and satirical pieces; when, in 1694, Molesworth published his "Account of Denmark," in which he treats the Danes and their monarch with great contempt; and takes the opportunity of insinuating those wild principles by which he supposes liberty to be established, and by which his adversaries suspect that all subordination and government is endangered.

This book offended Prince George; and the Danish Minister presented a memorial against it. The principles of its author did not please Dr. King; and therefore he undertook to confute part, and laugh at the rest. The controversy is now forgotten: and books of this kind seldom live long when interest and resentment have ceased.

In 1697 he mingled in the controversy between Boyle and Bentley; and was one of those who tried what wit could perform in opposition to learning, on a question which learning only could decide.

In 1699 was published by him "A Journey to London," after the method of Dr. Martin Lister, who had published "A Journey to Paris." And in 1700 he satirised the Royal Society—at least, Sir Hans Sloane, their president—in two dialogues, intituled "The Transactioner."

Though he was a regular advocate in the courts of civil and canon law, he did not love his profession, nor, indeed, any kind of business which interrupted his voluptuary dreams or forced him to rouse from that indulgence in which only he could find delight. His reputation as a civilian was yet maintained by his judgments in the Courts of Delegates, and raised very high by the address and knowledge which he discovered in 1700, when he defended the Earl of Anglesea against his lady, afterwards Duchess of Buckinghamshire, who sued for a divorce and obtained it.

The expense of his pleasures, and neglect of business, had now lessened his revenues; and he was willing to accept of a settlement in Ireland, where, about 1702, he was made Judge of the Admiralty, Commissioner of the Prizes, Keeper of the Records in Birmingham's Tower, and Vicar–General to Dr. Marsh, the primate.

But it is vain to put wealth within the reach of him who will not stretch out his hand to take it. King soon found a friend, as idle and thoughtless as himself, in Upton, one of the judges, who had a pleasant house called Mountown, near Dublin, to which King frequently retired; delighting to neglect his interest, forget his cares, and desert his duty.

Here he wrote "Mully of Mountown," a poem; by which, though fanciful readers in the pride of sagacity have given it a poetical interpretation, was meant originally no more than it expressed, as it was dictated only by the author's delight in the quiet of Mountown.

In 1708, when Lord Wharton was sent to govern Ireland, King returned to London, with his poverty, his idleness, and his wit; and published some essays, called "Useful Transactions." His "Voyage to the Island of Cajamai" is particularly commended. He then wrote the "Art of Love," a poem remarkable, notwithstanding its title, for purity of sentiment; and in 1709 imitated Horace in an "Art of Cookery," which he published with some letters to Dr. Lister.

In 1710 he appeared as a lover of the Church, on the side of Sacheverell; and was supposed to have concurred at least in the projection of the Examiner. His eyes were open to all the operations of Whiggism; and he bestowed some strictures upon Dr. Kennet's adulatory sermon at the funeral of the Duke of Devonshire.

"The History of the Heathen Gods," a book composed for schools, was written by him in 1711. The work is useful, but might have been produced without the powers of King. The same year he published "Rufinus," an historical essay; and a poem intended to dispose the nation to think as he thought of the Duke of Marlborough and his adherents.

In 1711, competence, if not plenty, was again put into his power. He was, without the trouble of attendance or the mortification of a request, made Gazetteer. Swift, Freind, Prior, and other men of the same party, brought him the key of the Gazetteer's office. He was now again placed in a profitable employment, and again threw the benefit away. An Act of Insolvency made his business at that time particularly troublesome; and he would not wait till hurry should be at an end, but impatiently resigned it, and returned to his wonted indigence and amusements.

One of his amusements at Lambeth, where he resided, was to mortify Dr. Tenison, the archbishop, by a public festivity on the surrender of Dunkirk to Hill; an event with which Tenison's political bigotry did not suffer him to be delighted. King was resolved to counteract his sullenness, and at the expense of a few barrels of ale filled the neighbourhood with honest merriment.

In the autumn of 1712 his health declined; he grew weaker by degrees, and died on Christmas Day. Though his life had not been without irregularity, his principles were pure and orthodox, and his death was pious.

After this relation it will be naturally supposed that his poems were rather the amusements of idleness than efforts of study; that he endeavoured rather to divert than astonish; that his thoughts seldom aspired to sublimity; and that, if his verse was easy and his images familiar, he attained what he desired. His purpose is to be merry; but perhaps, to enjoy his mirth, it may be sometimes necessary to think well of his opinions.

HALIFAX.

The life of the Earl of Halifax was properly that of an artful and active statesman, employed in balancing parties, contriving expedients, and combating opposition, and exposed to the vicissitudes of advancement and degradation; but in this collection poetical merit is the claim to attention; and the account which is here to be expected may properly be proportioned, not to his influence in the State, but to his rank among the writers of verse.

Charles Montague was born April 16, 1661, at Horton, in Northamptonshire, the son of Mr. George Montague, a younger son of the Earl of Manchester. He was educated first in the country, and then removed to Westminster, where, in 1677, he was chosen a King's Scholar, and recommended himself to Busby by his felicity in extemporary epigrams. He contracted a very intimate friendship with Mr. Stepney; and in 1682, when Stepney was elected at Cambridge, the election of Montague being not to proceed till the year following, he was afraid lest by being placed at Oxford he might be separated from his companion, and therefore solicited to be removed to Cambridge, without waiting for the advantages of another year.

It seemed indeed time to wish for a removal, for he was already a schoolboy of one–and–twenty.

His relation, Dr. Montague, was then Master of the college in which he was placed a Fellow–Commoner, and took him under his particular care. Here he commenced an acquaintance with the great Newton, which continued through his life, and was at last attested by a legacy.

In 1685 his verses on the death of King Charles made such an impression on the Earl of Dorset that he was invited to town, and introduced by that universal patron to the other wits. In 1687 he joined with Prior in "The City Mouse and the Country Mouse," a burlesque of Dryden's "Hind and Panther." He signed the invitation to the Prince of Orange, and sat in the Convention. He about the same time married the Countess Dowager of Manchester, and intended to have taken Orders; but, afterwards altering his purpose, he purchased for 1,500 pounds the place of one of the clerks of the Council.

After he had written his epistle on the victory of the Boyne, his patron Dorset introduced him to King William with this expression, "Sir, I have brought a MOUSE to wait on your Majesty." To which the King is said to have replied, "You do well to put me in the way of making a MAN of him;" and ordered him a pension of 500 pounds. This story, however current, seems to have been made after the event. The King's answer implies a greater acquaintance with our proverbial and familiar diction than King William could possibly have attained.

In 1691, being member of the House of Commons, he argued warmly in favour of a law to grant the assistance of counsel in trials for high treason; and in the midst of his speech falling into some confusion, was for a while silent; but, recovering himself, observed, "how reasonable it was to allow counsel to men called as criminals before a court of justice, when it appeared how much the presence of that assembly could disconcert one of their own body."

After this he rose fast into honours and employments, being made one of the Commissioners of the Treasury, and called to the Privy Council. In 1694 he became Chancellor of the Exchequer; and the next year engaged in the great attempt of the recoinage, which was in two years happily completed. In 1696 he projected the GENERAL FUND and raised the credit of the Exchequer; and after inquiry concerning a grant of Irish Crown lands, it was determined by a vote of the Commons that Charles Montague, Esq., HAD DESERVED HIS MAJESTY'S FAVOUR. In 1698, being advanced to the first Commission of the Treasury, he was appointed one of the regency in the King's absence: the next year he was made Auditor of the Exchequer, and the year after created Baron Halifax. He was, however, impeached by the Commons; but the Articles were dismissed by the Lords.

At the accession of Queen Anne he was dismissed from the Council; and in the first Parliament of her reign was again attacked by the Commons, and again escaped by the protection of the Lords. In 1704 he wrote an answer to Bromley's speech against occasional conformity. He headed the inquiry into the danger of the Church. In 1706 he proposed and negotiated the Union with Scotland; and when the Elector of Hanover received the Garter, after the Act had passed for securing the Protestant Succession, he was appointed to carry the ensigns of the Order to the Electoral Court. He sat as one of the judges of Sacheverell, but voted for a mild sentence. Being now no longer in favour, he contrived to obtain a writ for summoning the Electoral Prince to Parliament as Duke of Cambridge.

At the Queen's death he was appointed one of the regents; and at the accession of George I. was made Earl of Halifax, Knight of the Garter, and First Commissioner of the Treasury, with a grant to his nephew of the reversion of the Auditorship of the Exchequer. More was not to be had, and this he kept but a little while; for on the 19th of May, 1715, he died of an inflammation of his lungs.

Of him, who from a poet became a patron of poets, it will be readily believed that the works would not miss of celebration. Addison began to praise him early, and was followed or accompanied by other poets; perhaps by almost all, except Swift and Pope, who forbore to flatter him in his life, and after his death spoke of him—Swift with slight censure, and Pope, in the character of Bufo, with acrimonious contempt.

He was, as Pope says, "fed with dedications;" for Tickell affirms that no dedication was unrewarded. To charge all unmerited praise with the guilt of flattery, and to suppose that the encomiast always knows and feels the falsehoods of his assertions, is surely to discover great ignorance of human nature and human life. In determinations depending not on rules, but on experience and comparison, judgment is always in some degree subject to affection. Very near to admiration is the wish to admire.

Every man willingly gives value to the praise which he receives, and considers the sentence passed in his favour as the sentence of discernment. We admire in a friend that understanding that selected us for confidence; we admire more, in a patron, that judgment which, instead of scattering bounty indiscriminately, directed it to us; and, if the patron be an author, those performances which gratitude forbids us to blame, affection will easily dispose us to exalt.

To these prejudices, hardly culpable, interest adds a power always operating, though not always, because not willingly, perceived. The modesty of praise wears gradually away; and perhaps the pride of patronage may be in time so increased that modest praise will no longer please.

Many a blandishment was practised upon Halifax which he would never have known had he no other attractions than those of his poetry, of which a short time has withered the beauties. It would now be esteemed no honour, by a contributor to the monthly bundles of verses, to be told that, in strains either familiar or solemn, he sings like Montague.

PARNELL.

The life of Dr. Parnell is a task which I should very willingly decline, since it has been lately written by Goldsmith, a man of such variety of powers, and such felicity of performance, that he always seemed to do best that which he was doing; a man who had the art of being minute without tediousness, and general without confusion; whose language was copious without exuberance, exact without constraint, and easy without weakness.

What such an author has told, who would tell again? I have made an abstract from his larger narrative; and have this gratification from my attempt, that it gives me an opportunity of paying due tribute to the memory of Goldsmith.

Thomas Parnell was the son of a Commonwealthsman of the same name, who, at the Restoration, left Congleton, in Cheshire, where the family had been established for several centuries, and, settling in Ireland, purchased an estate, which, with his lands in Cheshire, descended to the poet, who was born at Dublin in 1679; and, after the usual education at a grammar school, was, at the age of thirteen, admitted into the College where, in 1700, he became Master of Arts; and was the same year ordained a deacon, though under the canonical age, by a dispensation from the Bishop of Derry.

About three years afterwards he was made a priest and in 1705 Dr. Ashe, the Bishop of Clogher, conferred upon him the archdeaconry of Clogher. About the same time he married Mrs. Anne Minchin, an amiable lady, by whom he had two sons, who died young, and a daughter, who long survived him.

At the ejection of the Whigs, in the end of Queen Anne's reign, Parnell was persuaded to change his party, not without much censure from those whom he forsook, and was received by the new Ministry as a valuable reinforcement. When the Earl of Oxford was told that Dr. Parnell waited among the crowd in the outer room, he went, by the persuasion of Swift, with his Treasurer's staff in his hand, to inquire for him, and to bid him welcome; and, as may be inferred from Pope's dedication, admitted him as a favourite companion to his convivial hours, but, as it seems often to have happened in those times to the favourites of the great, without attention to his fortune, which, however, was in no great need of improvement.

Parnell, who did not want ambition or vanity, was desirous to make himself conspicuous, and to show how worthy he was of high preferment. As he thought himself qualified to become a popular preacher, he displayed his elocution with great success in the pulpits of London; but the Queen's death putting an end to his expectations, abated his diligence; and Pope represents him as falling from that time into intemperance of wine. That in his latter life he was too much a lover of the bottle, is not denied; but I have heard it imputed to a cause more likely to obtain forgiveness from mankind, the untimely death of a darling son; or, as others tell, the loss of his wife, who died (1712) in the midst of his expectations.

He was now to derive every future addition to his preferments from his personal interest with his private friends, and he was not long unregarded. He was warmly recommended by Swift to Archbishop King, who gave him a prebend in 1713; and in May, 1716, presented him to the vicarage of Finglass, in the diocese of Dublin, worth 400 pounds a year. Such notice from such a man inclines me to believe that the vice of which he has been accused was not gross or not notorious.

But his prosperity did not last long. His end, whatever was its cause, was now approaching. He enjoyed his preferment little more than a year; for in July, 1717, in his thirty–eighth year, he died at Chester on his way to Ireland.

He seems to have been one of those poets who take delight in writing. He contributed to the papers of that time, and probably published more than he owned. He left many compositions behind him, of which Pope selected those which he thought best, and dedicated them to the Earl of Oxford. Of these Goldsmith has given an opinion, and his criticism it is seldom safe to contradict. He bestows just praise upon "The Rise of Woman," "The Fairy Tale," and "The Pervigilium Veneris;" but has very properly remarked that in "The Battle of Mice and Frogs" the Greek names have not in English their original effect. He tells us that "The Bookworm" is borrowed from Beza; but he should have added with modern applications: and when he discovers that "Gay Bacchus" is translated from Augurellus, he ought to have remarked that the latter part is purely Parnell's. Another poem, "When Spring Comes On," is, he says, taken from the French. I would add that the description of "Barrenness," in his verses to Pope, was borrowed from

Secundus; but lately searching for the passage which I had formerly read, I could not find it. "The Night Piece on Death" is indirectly preferred by Goldsmith to Gray's "Churchyard;" but, in my opinion, Gray has the advantage in dignity, variety, and originality of sentiment. He observes that the story of "The Hermit" is in More's "Dialogues" and Howell's "Letters," and supposes it to have been originally Arabian.

Goldsmith has not taken any notice of "The Elegy to the Old Beauty," which is perhaps the meanest; nor of "The Allegory on Man," the happiest of Parnell's performances. The hint of "The Hymn to Contentment" I suspect to have been borrowed from Cleveland.

The general character of Parnell is not great extent of comprehension or fertility of mind. Of the little that appears, still less is his own. His praise must be derived from the easy sweetness of his diction: in his verses there is more happiness than pains; he is sprightly without effort, and always delights, though he never ravishes; everything is proper, yet everything seems casual. If there is some appearance of elaboration in "The Hermit," the narrative, as it is less airy, is less pleasing. Of his other compositions it is impossible to say whether they are the productions of nature, so excellent as not to want the help of art, or of art so refined as to resemble nature.

This criticism relates only to the pieces published by Pope. Of the large appendages which I find in the last edition, I can only say that I know not whence they came, nor have ever inquired whither they are going. They stand upon the faith of the compilers.

GARTH.

Samuel Garth was of a good family in Yorkshire, and from some school in his own county became a student at Peter House, in Cambridge, where he resided till he became Doctor of Physic on July the 7th, 1691. He was examined before the College at London on March the 12th, 1691–2, and admitted Fellow June 26th, 1693. He was soon so much distinguished by his conversation and accomplishments as to obtain very extensive practice; and, if a pamphlet of those times may be credited, had the favour and confidence of one party, as Radcliffe had of the other. He is always mentioned as a man of benevolence; and it is just to suppose that his desire of helping the helpless disposed him to so much zeal for "The Dispensary;" an undertaking of which some account, however short, is proper to be given.

Whether what Temple says be true, that physicians have had more learning than the other faculties, I will not stay to inquire; but I believe every man has found in physicians great liberality and dignity of sentiment, very prompt effusion of beneficence, and willingness to exert a lucrative art where there is no hope of lucre. Agreeably to this character, the College of Physicians, in July, 1687, published an edict, requiring all the Fellows, Candidates, and Licentiates to give gratuitous advice to the neighbouring poor. This edict was sent to the Court of Aldermen; and, a question being made to whom the appellation of the POOR should be extended, the College answered that it should be sufficient to bring a testimonial from the clergyman officiating in the parish where the patient resided.

After a year's experience the physicians found their charity frustrated by some malignant opposition, and made to a great degree vain by the high price of physic; they therefore voted, in August, 1688, that the laboratory of the College should be accommodated to the preparation of medicines, and another room prepared for their reception; and that the contributors to the expense should manage the charity.

It was now expected that the apothecaries would have undertaken the care of providing medicines; but they took another course. Thinking the whole design pernicious to their interest, they endeavoured to raise a faction against it in the College, and found some physicians mean enough to solicit their patronage by betraying to them the counsels of the College. The greater part, however, enforced by a new edict, in 1694, the former order of 1687, and sent it to the Mayor and Aldermen, who appointed a committee to treat with the College and settle the mode of administering the charity.

It was desired by the aldermen that the testimonials of churchwardens and overseers should be admitted; and that all hired servants, and all apprentices to handicraftsmen, should be considered as POOR. This likewise was granted by the College.

It was then considered who should distribute the medicines, and who should settle their prices. The physicians procured some apothecaries to undertake the dispensation, and offered that the warden and company of the apothecaries should adjust the price. This offer was rejected; and the apothecaries who had engaged to assist the charity were considered as traitors to the company, threatened with the imposition of troublesome offices, and deterred from the performance of their engagements. The apothecaries ventured upon public opposition, and presented a kind of remonstrance against the design to the committee of the City, which the physicians condescended to confute: and at last the traders seem to have prevailed among the sons of trade; for the proposal of the College having been considered, a paper of approbation was drawn up, but postponed and forgotten.

The physicians still persisted; and in 1696 a subscription was raised by themselves according to an agreement prefixed to "The Dispensary." The poor were, for a time, supplied with medicines; for how long a time I know not. The medicinal charity, like others, began with ardour, but soon remitted, and at last died gradually away.

About the time of the subscription begins the action of "The Dispensary." The poem, as its subject was present and popular, co- operated with passions and prejudices then prevalent, and, with such auxiliaries to its intrinsic merit, was universally and liberally applauded. It was on the side of charity against the intrigues of interest; and of regular learning against licentious usurpation of medical authority, and was therefore naturally favoured by those who read and can judge of poetry.

In 1697 Garth spoke that which is now called "The Harveian Oration;" which the authors of "The Biographia" mention with more praise than the passage quoted in their notes will fully justify. Garth, speaking of the mischiefs done by quacks, has these expressions: "Non tamen telis vulnerat ista agyrtarum colluvies, sed theriaca quadam magis perniciosa, non pyrio, sed pulvere nescio quo exotico certat, non globulis plumbeis, sed pilulis aeque lethalibus interficit." This was certainly thought fine by the author, and is still admired by his biographer. In October, 1702, he became one of the censors of the College,

Garth, being an active and zealous Whig, was a member of the Kit-Cat Club, and, by consequence, familiarly known to all the great men of that denomination. In 1710, when the government fell into other hands, he writ to Lord Godolphin, on his dismission, a short poem, which was criticised in the Examiner, and so successfully either defended or excused by Mr. Addison that, for the sake of the vindication, it ought to be preserved.

At the accession of the present family his merits were acknowledged and rewarded. He was knighted with the sword of his hero, Marlborough; and was made Physician-in-Ordinary to the King, and Physician-General to the army. He then undertook an edition of Ovid's "Metamorphoses," translated by several hands; which he recommended by a preface, written with more ostentation than ability; his notions are half–formed, and his materials immethodically confused. This was his last work. He died January 18th, 1717–18, and was buried at Harrow–on–the–Hill.

His personal character seems to have been social and liberal. He communicated himself through a very wide extent of acquaintance; and though firm in a party, at a time when firmness included virulence, yet he imparted his kindness to those who were not supposed to favour his principles. He was an early encourager of Pope, and was at once the friend of Addison and of Granville. He is accused of voluptuousness and irreligion; and Pope, who says that "if ever there was a good Christian, without knowing himself to be so, it was Dr. Garth," seems not able to deny what he is angry to hear and loth to confess.

Pope afterwards declared himself convinced that Garth died in the communion of the Church of Rome, having been privately reconciled. It is observed by Lowth that there is less distance than is thought between scepticism and Popery; and that a mind wearied with perpetual doubt, willingly seeks repose in the bosom of an infallible Church.

His poetry has been praised at least equally to its merit. In "The Dispensary" there is a strain of smooth and free versification; but few lines are eminently elegant. No passages fall below mediocrity, and few rise much above it. The plan seems formed without just proportion to the subject; the means and end have no necessary connection. Resnel, in his preface to Pope's Essay, remarks that Garth exhibits no discrimination of characters; and that what any one says might, with equal propriety, have been said by another. The general design is, perhaps, open to criticism; but the composition can seldom be charged with inaccuracy or negligence. The author never slumbers in self–indulgence; his full vigour is always exerted; scarcely a line is left unfinished; nor is it easy to find an expression used by constraint, or a thought imperfectly expressed. It was remarked by Pope, that "The Dispensary" had been corrected in every edition, and that every change was an improvement. It appears, however, to want something of poetical ardour, and something of general delectation; and therefore, since it has been no longer supported by accidental and intrinsic popularity, it has been scarcely able to support itself.

ROWE.

Nicholas Rowe was born at Little Beckford, in Bedfordshire, in 1673. His family had long possessed a considerable estate, with a good house, at Lambertoun in Devonshire. The ancestor from whom he descended in a direct line received the arms borne by his descendants for his bravery in the Holy War. His father, John Rowe, who was the first that quitted his paternal acres to practise any part of profit, professed the law, and published Benlow's and Dallison's Reports in the reign of James the Second, when, in opposition to the notions then diligently propagated of dispensing power, he ventured to remark how low his authors rated the prerogative. He was made a serjeant, and died April 30, 1692. He was buried in the Temple church.

Nicholas was first sent to a private school at Highgate; and, being afterwards removed to Westminster, was at twelve years chosen one of the King's Scholars. His master was Busby, who suffered none of his scholars to let their powers lie useless; and his exercises in several languages are said to have been written with uncommon degrees of excellence, and yet to have cost him very little labour. At sixteen he had, in his father's opinion, made advances in learning sufficient to qualify him for the study of law, and was entered a student of the Middle Temple, where for some time he read statutes and reports with proficiency proportionate to the force of his mind, which was already such that he endeavoured to comprehend law, not as a series of precedents, or collection of positive precepts, but as a system of rational government and impartial justice. When he was nineteen, he was, by the death of his father, left more to his own direction, and probably from that time suffered law gradually to give way to poetry. At twenty–five he produced the Ambitious Step–Mother, which was received with so much favour that he devoted himself from that time wholly to elegant literature.

His next tragedy (1702) was Tamerlane, in which, under the name of Tamerlane, he intended to characterise King William, and Louis the Fourteenth under Bajazet. The virtues of Tamerlane seem to have been arbitrarily assigned him by his poet, for I know not that history gives any other qualities than those which make a conqueror. The fashion, however, of the time was to accumulate upon Louis all that can raise horror and detestation; and whatever good was withheld from him, that it might not be thrown away was bestowed upon King William. This was the tragedy which Rowe valued most, and that which probably, by the help of political auxiliaries, excited most applause; but occasional poetry must often content itself with occasional praise. Tamerlane has for a long time been acted only once a year, on the night when King William landed. Our quarrel with Louis has been long over; and it now gratifies neither zeal nor malice to see him painted with aggravated features, like a Saracen upon a sign.

15

Lives of the Poets

The Fair Penitent, his next production (1703), is one of the most pleasing tragedies on the stage, where it still keeps its turns of appearing, and probably will long keep them, for there is scarcely any work of any poet at once so interesting by the fable, and so delightful by the language. The story is domestic, and therefore easily received by the imagination, and assimilated to common life; the diction is exquisitely harmonious, and soft or sprightly as occasion requires.

The character of Lothario seems to have been expanded by Richardson into Lovelace; but he has excelled his original in the moral effect of the fiction. Lothario, with gaiety which cannot be hated, and bravery which cannot be despised, retains too much of the spectator's kindness. It was in the power of Richardson alone to teach us at once esteem and detestation, to make virtuous resentment overpower all the benevolence which wit, elegance, and courage, naturally excite; and to lose at last the hero in the villain. The fifth act is not equal to the former; the events of the drama are exhausted, and little remains but to talk of what is past. It has been observed that the title of the play does not sufficiently correspond with the behaviour of Calista, who at last shows no evident signs of repentance, but may be reasonably suspected of feeling pain from detection rather than from guilt, and expresses more shame than sorrow, and more rage than shame.

His next (1706) was Ulysses; which, with the common fate of mythological stories, is now generally neglected. We have been too early acquainted with the poetical heroes to expect any pleasure from their revival; to show them as they have already been shown, is to disgust by repetition; to give them new qualities, or new adventures, is to offend by violating received notions.

"The Royal Convert" (1708) seems to have a better claim to longevity. The fable is drawn from an obscure and barbarous age, to which fictions are more easily and properly adapted; for when objects are imperfectly seen, they easily take forms from imagination. The scene lies among our ancestors in our own country, and therefore very easily catches attention. Rodogune is a personage truly tragical, of high spirit, and violent passions, great with tempestuous dignity, and wicked with a soul that would have been heroic if it had been virtuous. The motto seems to tell that this play was not successful.

Rowe does not always remember what his characters require. In Tamerlane there is some ridiculous mention of the God of Love; and Rodogune, a savage Saxon, talks of Venus and the eagle that bears the thunder of Jupiter.

This play discovers its own date, by a prediction of the Union, in imitation of Cranmer's prophetic promises to Henry VIII. The anticipated blessings of union are not very naturally introduced, nor very happily expressed. He once (1706) tried to change his hand. He ventured on a comedy, and produced the Biter, with which, though it was unfavourably treated by the audience, he was himself delighted; for he is said to have sat in the house laughing with great vehemence, whenever he had, in his own opinion, produced a jest. But finding that he and the public had no sympathy of mirth, he tried at lighter scenes no more.

After the Royal Convert (1714) appeared Jane Shore, written, as its author professes, IN IMITATION OF SHAKESPEARE'S STYLE. In what he thought himself an imitator of Shakespeare it is not easy to conceive. The numbers, the diction, the sentiments, and the conduct, everything in which imitation can consist, are remote in the utmost degree from the manner of Shakespeare, whose dramas it resembles only as it is an English story, and as some of the persons have their names in history. This play, consisting chiefly of domestic scenes and private distress, lays hold upon the heart. The wife is forgiven because she repents, and the husband is honoured because he forgives. This, therefore, is one of those pieces which we still welcome on the stage.

His last tragedy (1715) was Lady Jane Grey. This subject had been chosen by Mr. Smith, whose papers were put into Rowe's hands such as he describes them in his preface. This play has likewise sunk into oblivion. From this time he gave nothing more to the stage.

Being by a competent fortune exempted from any necessity of combating his inclination, he never wrote in distress, and therefore does not appear to have ever written in haste. His works were finished to his own approbation, and bear few marks of negligence or hurry. It is remarkable that his prologues and epilogues are all his own, though he sometimes supplied others; he afforded help, but did not solicit it.

As his studies necessarily made him acquainted with Shakespeare, and acquaintance produced veneration, he undertook (1709) an edition of his works, from which he neither received much praise, nor seems to have expected it; yet I believe those who compare it with former copies will find that he has done more than he promised; and that, without the pomp of notes or boasts of criticism, many passages are happily restored. He prefixed a life of the author, such as tradition, then almost expiring, could supply, and a preface, which cannot be said to discover much profundity or penetration. He at least contributed to the popularity of his author. He was willing enough to improve his fortune by other arts than poetry. He was under–secretary for three years when the Duke of Queensberry was Secretary of State, and afterwards applied to the Earl of Oxford for some public employment. Oxford enjoined him to study Spanish; and when, some time afterwards, he came again, and said that he had mastered it, dismissed him with this congratulation, "Then, sir, I envy you the pleasure of reading 'Don Quixote' in the original."

This story is sufficiently attested; but why Oxford, who desired to be thought a favourer of literature, should thus insult a man of acknowledged merit, or how Rowe, who was so keen a Whig that he did not willingly converse with men of the opposite party, could ask preferment from Oxford, it is not now possible to discover. Pope, who told the story, did not say on what occasion the advice was given; and, though he owned Rowe's disappointment, doubted whether any injury was intended him, but thought it rather Lord Oxford's ODD WAY.

It is likely that he lived on discontented through the rest of Queen Anne's reign; but the time came at last when he found kinder friends. At the accession of King George he was made Poet–Laureate– –I am afraid, by the ejection of poor Nahum Tate, who (1716) died in the Mint, where he was forced to seek shelter by extreme poverty. He was made likewise one of the land–surveyors of the customs of the Port of London. The Prince of Wales chose him Clerk of his Council; and the Lord Chancellor Parker, as soon as he received the seals, appointed him, unasked, Secretary of the Presentations. Such an accumulation of employments undoubtedly produced a very considerable revenue.

Having already translated some parts of Lucan's "Pharsalia," which had been published in the Miscellanies, and doubtless received many praises, he undertook a version of the whole work, which he lived to finish, but not to publish. It seems to have been printed under the care of Dr. Welwood, who prefixed the author's life, in which is contained the following character:—

"As to his person, it was graceful and well made; his face regular, and of a manly beauty. As his soul was well lodged, so its rational and animal faculties excelled in a high degree. He had a quick and fruitful invention, a deep penetration, and a large compass of thought, with singular dexterity and easiness in making his thoughts to be understood. He was master of most parts of polite learning, especially the classical authors, both Greek and Latin; understood the French, Italian, and Spanish languages, and spoke the first fluently, and the other two tolerably well. He had likewise read most of the Greek and Roman histories in their original languages, and most that are wrote in English, French, Italian, and Spanish. He had a good taste in philosophy; and, having a firm impression of religion upon his mind, he took great delight in divinity and ecclesiastical history, in both of which he made great advances in the times he retired into the country, which was frequent. He expressed on all occasions his full persuasion of the truth of revealed religion; and, being a sincere member of the Established Church himself, he pitied, but condemned not, those that dissented from it. He abhorred the principles of persecuting men upon the account of their opinions in religion; and, being strict in his own, he took it not upon him to censure those of another persuasion. His conversation was pleasant, witty, and learned, without the least tincture of affectation or pedantry; and his inimitable manner of diverting and enlivening the company made it impossible for any one to be out of humour when he was in it. Envy and detraction seemed to be entirely foreign to his constitution; and whatever provocations he met with at any time, he passed them over without the least thought of resentment or revenge. As Homer had a Zoilus, so Mr. Rowe had sometimes his; for there were not wanting malevolent people, and pretenders to poetry too, that would now and then bark at his best performances; but he was so conscious of his own genius, and had so much good–nature, as to forgive them, nor could he ever be tempted to return them an answer.

"The love of learning and poetry made him not the less fit for business, and nobody applied himself closer to it when it required his attendance. The late Duke of Queensberry, when he was Secretary of State, made him his secretary for public affairs; and when that truly great man came to know him well, he was never so pleased as when Mr. Rowe was in his company. After the duke's death, all avenues were stopped to his preferment; and during the rest of that reign he passed his time with the Muses and his books, and sometimes the conversation of his friends. When he had just got to be easy in his fortune, and was in a fair way to make it better, death swept him away, and in him deprived the world of one of the best men, as well as one of the best geniuses, of the age. He died like a Christian and a philosopher, in charity with all mankind, and with an absolute resignation to the will of God. He kept up his good– humour to the last; and took leave of his wife and friends, immediately before his last agony, with the same tranquillity of mind, and the same indifference for life, as though he had been upon taking but a short journey. He was twice married—first to a daughter of Mr. Parsons, one of the auditors of the revenue; and afterwards to a daughter of Mr. Devenish, of a good family in Dorsetshire. By the first he had a son; and by the second a daughter, married afterwards to Mr. Fane. He died 6th December, 1718, in the forty–fifth year of his age, and was buried on the 19th of the same month in Westminster Abbey, in the aisle where many of our English poets are interred, over against Chaucer, his body being attended by a select number of his friends, and the dean and choir officiating at the funeral."

To this character, which is apparently given with the fondness of a friend, may be added the testimony of Pope, who says, in a letter to Blount, "Mr. Rowe accompanied me, and passed a week in the Forest. I need not tell you how much a man of his turn entertained me; but I must acquaint you, there is a vivacity and gaiety of disposition, almost peculiar to him, which make it impossible to part from him without that uneasiness which generally succeeds all our pleasure."

Pope has left behind him another mention of his companion less advantageous, which is thus reported by Dr. Warburton:—

"Rowe, in Mr. Pope's opinion, maintained a decent character, but had no heart. Mr. Addison was justly offended with some behaviour which arose from that want, and estranged himself from him, which Rowe felt very severely. Mr. Pope, their common friend, knowing this, took an opportunity, at some juncture of Mr. Addison's advancement, to tell him how poor Rowe was grieved at his displeasure, and what satisfaction he expressed at Mr. Addison's good fortune, which he expressed so naturally that he (Mr. Pope) could not but think him sincere. Mr. Addison replied, 'I do not suspect that he feigned; but the levity of his heart is such, that he is struck with any new adventure, and it would affect him just in the same manner if he heard I was going to be hanged.' Mr. Pope said he could not deny but Mr. Addison understood Rowe well."

This censure time has not left us the power of confirming or refuting; but observation daily shows that much stress is not to be laid on hyperbolical accusations and pointed sentences, which even he that utters them desires to be applauded rather than credited. Addison can hardly be supposed to have meant all that he said. Few characters can bear the microscopic scrutiny of wit quickened by anger; and, perhaps, the best advice to authors would be, that they should keep out of the way of one another.

Rowe is chiefly to be considered as a tragic writer and a translator. In his attempt at comedy he failed so ignominiously that his Biter is not inserted in his works: and his occasional poems and short compositions are rarely worthy either praise or censure, for they seem the casual sports of a mind seeking rather to amuse its leisure than to exercise its powers. In the construction of his dramas there is not much art; he is not a nice observer of the unities. He extends time and varies places as his convenience requires. To vary the place is not, in my opinion, any violation of nature, if the change be made between the acts, for it is no less easy for the spectator to suppose himself at Athens in the second act, than at Thebes in the first; but to change the scene, as is done by Rowe, in the middle of an act, is to add more acts to the play, since an act is so much of the business as is transacted without interruption. Rowe, by this licence, easily extricates himself from difficulties; as in Jane Grey, when we have been terrified with all the dreadful pomp of public execution; and are wondering how the heroine or the poet will proceed, no sooner has Jane pronounced some prophetic rhymes than—pass and be gone—the scene closes, and Pembroke and Gardiner are turned out upon the stage.

I know not that there can be found in his plays any deep search into nature, any accurate discriminations of kindred qualities, or nice display of passion in its progress; all is general and undefined. Nor does he much interest or affect the auditor, except in Jane Shore, who is always seen and heard with pity. Alicia is a character of empty noise, with no resemblance to real sorrow or to natural madness.

Whence, then, has Rowe his reputation? From the reasonableness and propriety of some of his scenes, from the elegance of his diction, and the suavity of his verse. He seldom moves either pity or terror, but he often elevates the sentiments; he seldom pierces the breast, but he always delights the ear, and often improves the understanding. His translation of the "Golden Verses," and of the first book of Quillet's poem, have nothing in them remarkable. The "Golden Verses" are tedious.

The version of Lucan is one of the greatest productions of English poetry, for there is perhaps none that so completely exhibits the genius and spirit of the original. Lucan is distinguished by a kind of dictatorial or philosophic dignity, rather, as Quintilian observes, declamatory than poetical; full of ambitious morality and pointed sentences, comprised in vigorous and animated lines. This character Rowe has very diligently and successfully preserved. His versification, which is such as his contemporaries practised, without any attempt at innovation or improvement, seldom wants either melody or force. His author's sense is sometimes a little diluted by additional infusions, and sometimes weakened by too much expansion. But such faults are to be expected in all translations, from the constraint of measures and dissimilitude of languages. The "Pharsalia" of Rowe deserves more notice than it obtains, and as it is more read will be more esteemed.

GAY.

John Gay, descended from an old family that had been long in possession of the manor of Goldworthy, in Devonshire, was born in 1688, at or near Barnstaple, where he was educated by Mr. Luck, who taught the school of that town with good reputation, and, a little before he retired from it, published a volume of Latin and English verses. Under such a master he was likely to form a taste for poetry. Being born without prospect of hereditary riches, he was sent to London in his youth, and placed apprentice with a silk mercer. How long he continued behind the counter, or with what degree of softness and dexterity he received and accommodated the ladies, as he probably took no delight in telling it, is not known. The report is that he was soon weary of either the restraint or servility of his occupation, and easily persuaded his master to discharge him.

The Duchess of Monmouth, remarkable for inflexible perseverance in her demand to be treated as a princess, in 1712 took Gay into her service as secretary: by quitting a shop for such service he might gain leisure, but he certainly advanced little in the boast of independence. Of his leisure he made so good use that he published next year a poem on "Rural Sports," and inscribed it to Mr. Pope, who was then rising fast into reputation. Pope was pleased with the honour, and when he became acquainted with Gay, found such attractions in his manners and conversation that he seems to have received him into his inmost confidence; and a friendship was formed between them which lasted to their separation by death, without any known abatement on either part. Gay was the general favourite of the whole association of wits; but they regarded him as a playfellow rather than a partner, and treated him with more fondness than respect.

Next year he published "The Shepherd's Week," six English pastorals, in which the images are drawn from real life, such as it appears among the rustics in parts of England remote from London. Steele, in some papers of the Guardian, had praised Ambrose Philips as the pastoral writer that yielded only to Theocritus, Virgil, and Spenser. Pope, who had also published pastorals, not pleased to be overlooked, drew up a comparison of his own compositions with those of Philips, in which he covertly gave himself the preference, while he seemed to disown it. Not content with this, he is supposed to have incited Gay to write "The Shepherd's Week," to show that, if it be necessary to copy nature with minuteness, rural life must be exhibited such as grossness and ignorance have made it. So far the plan was reasonable; but the pastorals are introduced by a Proeme, written with such imitation as they could attain of obsolete language, and, by consequence, in a style that was never spoken nor written in any language or in any place. But the effect of reality and truth became conspicuous, even when the intention was to show them grovelling and degraded. These pastorals became popular, and were read with delight as just representations of rural manners and occupations by those who had no interest in the rivalry of the poets, nor knowledge of the critical dispute.

In 1713 he brought a comedy called The Wife of Bath upon the stage, but it received no applause; he printed it, however, and seventeen years after, having altered it and, as he thought, adapted it more to the public taste, he offered it again to the town; but, though he was flushed with the success of the Beggar's Opera, had the mortification to see it again rejected.

In the last year of Queen Anne's life Gay was made secretary to the Earl of Clarendon, Ambassador to the Court of Hanover. This was a station that naturally gave him hopes of kindness from every party; but the Queen's death put an end to her favours, and he had dedicated his "Shepherd's Week" to Bolingbroke, which Swift considered as the crime that obstructed all kindness from the House of Hanover. He did not, however, omit to improve the right which his office had given him to the notice of the Royal Family. On the arrival of the Princess of Wales he wrote a poem, and obtained so much favour that both the Prince and the Princess went to see his What D'ye Call It, a kind of mock tragedy, in which the images were comic and the action grave; so that, as Pope relates, Mr. Cromwell, who could not hear what was said, was at a loss how to reconcile the laughter of the audience with the solemnity of the scene.

Of this performance the value certainly is but little; but it was one of the lucky trifles that give pleasure by novelty, and was so much favoured by the audience that envy appeared against it in the form of criticism; and Griffin, a player, in conjunction with Mr. Theobald, a man afterwards more remarkable, produced a pamphlet called "The Key to the What D'ye Call It," "which," says Gay, "calls me a blockhead, and Mr. Pope a knave."

But fortune has always been inconstant. Not long afterwards (1717) he endeavoured to entertain the town with Three Hours after Marriage, a comedy written, as there is sufficient reason for believing, by the joint assistance of Pope and Arbuthnot. One purpose of it was to bring into contempt Dr. Woodward, the fossilist, a man not really or justly contemptible. It had the fate which such outrages deserve. The scene in which Woodward was directly and apparently ridiculed, by the introduction of a mummy and a crocodile, disgusted the audience, and the performance was driven off the stage with general condemnation.

Gay is represented as a man easily incited to hope, and deeply depressed when his hopes were disappointed. This is not the character of a hero, but it may naturally imply something more generally welcome, a soft and civil companion. Whoever is apt to hope good from others is diligent to please them; but he that believes his powers strong enough to force their own way, commonly tries only to please himself. He had been simple enough to imagine that those who laughed at the What D'ye Call It would raise the fortune of its author, and, finding nothing done, sunk into dejection. His friends endeavoured to divert him. The Earl of Burlington sent him (1716) into Devonshire, the year after Mr. Pulteney took him to Aix, and in the following year Lord Harcourt invited him to his seat, where, during his visit, two rural lovers were killed with lightning, as is particularly told in Pope's "Letters."

Being now generally known, he published (1720) his poems by subscription, with such success that he raised a thousand pounds, and called his friends to a consultation what use might be best made of it. Lewis, the steward of Lord Oxford, advised him to intrust it to the Funds, and live upon the interest; Arbuthnot bade him to intrust it to Providence, and live upon the principal; Pope directed him, and was seconded by Swift, to purchase an annuity.

Gay in that disastrous year had a present from young Craggs of some South Sea Stock, and once supposed himself to be master of twenty thousand pounds. His friends persuaded him to sell his share; but he dreamed of dignity and splendour, and could not bear to obstruct his own fortune. He was then importuned to sell as much as would purchase a hundred a year for life, "which," says Penton, "will make you sure of a clean shirt and a shoulder of mutton every day." This counsel was rejected; the profit and principal were lost, and Gay sunk under the calamity so low that his life became in danger. By the care of his friends, among whom Pope appears to have shown particular tenderness, his health was restored; and, returning to his studies, he wrote a tragedy called The Captives, which he was invited to read before the Princess of Wales. When the hour came, he saw the Princess and her ladies all in expectation, and, advancing with reverence too great for any other attention, stumbled at a stool, and, falling forwards, threw down a weighty Japan screen. The Princess started, the ladies screamed, and poor Gay, after all the disturbance, was still to read his play.

The fate of The Captives, which was acted at Drury Lane in 1723–4, I know not; but he now thought himself in favour, and undertook (1726) to write a volume of "Fables" for the improvement of the young Duke of Cumberland. For this he is said to have been promised a reward, which he had doubtless magnified with all the wild expectations of indigence and vanity.

Next year the Prince and Princess became King and Queen, and Gay was to be great and happy; but on the settlement of the household, he found himself appointed gentleman usher to the Princess Louisa. By this offer he thought himself insulted, and sent a message to the Queen that he was too old for the place. There seem to have been many machinations employed afterwards in his favour, and diligent court was paid to Mrs. Howard, afterwards Countess of Suffolk, who was much beloved by the King and Queen, to engage her interest for his promotion; but solicitation, verses, and flatteries were thrown away; the lady heard them, and did nothing. All the pain which he suffered from neglect, or, as he perhaps termed it, the ingratitude of the Court, may be supposed to have been driven away by the unexampled success of the Beggar's Opera. This play, written in ridicule of the musical Italian drama, was first offered to Cibber and his brethren at Drury Lane and rejected: it being then carried to Rich, had the effect, as was ludicrously said, of making Gay RICH and Rich GAY. Of this lucky piece, as the reader cannot but wish to know the original and progress, I have inserted the relation which Spence has given in Pope's words:—

"Dr. Swift had been observing once to Mr. Gay what an odd pretty sort of a thing a Newgate Pastoral might make. Gay was inclined to try at such a thing for some time; but afterwards thought it would be better to write a comedy on the same plan. This was what gave rise to the Beggar's Opera. He began on it, and when first he mentioned it to Swift, the doctor did not much like the project. As he carried it on, he showed what he wrote to both of us, and we now and then gave a correction, or a word or two of advice; but it was wholly of his own writing. When it was done, neither of us thought it would succeed. We showed it to Congreve, who, after reading it over, said it would either take greatly or be damned confoundedly. We were all, at the first night of it, in great uncertainty of the event, till we were very much encouraged by overhearing the Duke of Argyll, who sat in the next box to us, say, 'It will do—it must do! I see it in the eyes of them.' This was a good while before the first act was over, and so gave us ease soon; for that Duke (besides his own good taste) has a particular knack, as any one now living, in discovering the taste of the public. He was quite right in this, as usual; the good–nature of the audience appeared stronger and stronger every act, and ended in a clamour of applause."

Its reception is thus recorded in the notes to the "Dunciad":—

"This piece was received with greater applause than was ever known. Besides being acted in London sixty–three days without interruption, and renewed the next season with equal applause, it spread into all the great towns of England; was played in many places to the thirtieth and fortieth time; at Bath and Bristol fifty, etc. It made its progress into Wales, Scotland, and Ireland, where it was performed twenty–four days successively. The ladies carried about with them the favourite songs of it in fans, and houses were furnished with it in screens. The fame of it was not confined to the author only. The person who acted Polly, till then obscure, became all at once the favourite of the town; her pictures were engraved and sold in great numbers; her life written, books of letters and verses to her published, and pamphlets made even of her sayings and jests. Furthermore, it drove out of England (for that season) the Italian Opera, which had carried all before it for ten years."

Of this performance, when it was printed, the reception was different, according to the different opinions of its readers. Swift commended it for the excellence of its morality, as a piece that "placed all kinds of vice in the strongest and most odious light;" but others, and among them Dr. Herring, afterwards Archbishop of Canterbury, censured it as giving encouragement, not only to vice, but to crimes, by making a highwayman the hero and dismissing him at last unpunished. It has been even said that after the exhibition of the Beggar's Opera the gangs of robbers were evidently multiplied.

Both these decisions are surely exaggerated. The play, like many others, was plainly written only to divert, without any moral purpose, and is therefore not likely to do good; nor can it be conceived, without more speculation than life requires or admits, to be productive of much evil. Highwaymen and housebreakers seldom frequent the playhouse, or mingle in any elegant diversion; nor is it possible for any one to imagine that he may rob with safety, because he sees Macheath reprieved upon the stage. This objection, however, or some other rather political than moral, obtained such prevalence that when

Gay produced a second part under the name of Polly, it was prohibited by the Lord Chamberlain; and he was forced to recompense his repulse by a subscription, which is said to have been so liberally bestowed that what he called oppression ended in profit. The publication was so much favoured that though the first part gained him four hundred pounds, near thrice as much was the profit of the second. He received yet another recompense for this supposed hardship, in the affectionate attention of the Duke and Duchess of Queensberry, into whose house he was taken, and with whom he passed the remaining part of his life. The Duke, considering his want of economy, undertook the management of his money, and gave it to him as he wanted it. But it is supposed that the discountenance of the Court sunk deep into his heart, and gave him more discontent than the applauses or tenderness of his friends could overpower. He soon fell into his old distemper, an habitual colic, and languished, though with many intervals of ease and cheerfulness, till a violent fit at last seized him and carried him to the grave, as Arbuthnot reported, with more precipitance than he had ever known. He died on the 4th of December, 1732, and was buried in Westminster Abbey. The letter which brought an account of his death to Swift, was laid by for some days unopened, because when he received it, he was impressed with the preconception of some misfortune.

After his death was published a second volume of "Fables," more political than the former. His opera of Achilles was acted, and the profits were given to two widow sisters, who inherited what he left, as his lawful heirs; for he died without a will, though he had gathered three thousand pounds. There have appeared likewise under his name a comedy called the Distressed Wife, and the Rehearsal at Gotham, a piece of humour.

The character given him by Pope is this, that "he was a natural man, without design, who spoke what he thought, and just as he thought it," and that "he was of a timid temper, and fearful of giving offence to the great;" which caution, however, says Pope, was of no avail.

As a poet he cannot be rated very high. He was, I once heard a female critic remark, "of a lower order." He had not in any great degree the MENS DIVINIOR, the dignity of genius. Much, however, must be allowed to the author of a new species of composition, though it be not of the highest kind. We owe to Gay the ballad opera, a mode of comedy which at first was supposed to delight only by its novelty, but has now, by the experience of half a century, been found so well accommodated to the disposition of a popular audience that it is likely to keep long possession of the stage. Whether this new drama was the product of judgment or of luck, the praise of it must be given to the inventor; and there are many writers read with more reverence to whom such merit or originality cannot be attributed.

His first performance, the Rural Sports, is such as was easily planned and executed; it is never contemptible, nor ever excellent. The Fan is one of those mythological fictions which antiquity delivers ready to the hand, but which, like other things that lie open to every one's use, are of little value. The attention naturally retires from a new tale of Venus, Diana, and Minerva.

His "Fables" seem to have been a favourite work; for, having published one volume, he left another behind him. Of this kind of Fables the author does not appear to have formed any distinct or settled notion. Phaedrus evidently confounds them with Tales, and Gay both with Tales and Allegorical Prosopopoeias. A Fable or Apologue, such as is now under consideration, seems to be, in its genuine state, a narrative in which beings irrational, and sometimes inanimate, arbores loquuntur, non tantum ferae, are, for the purpose of moral instruction, feigned to act and speak with human interests and passions. To this description the compositions of Gay do not always conform. For a fable he gives now and then a tale, or an abstracted allegory; and from some, by whatever name they may be called, it will be difficult to extract any moral principle. They are, however, told with liveliness, the versification is smooth, and the diction, though now and then a little constrained by the measure or the rhyme, is generally happy.

To "Trivia" may be allowed all that it claims; it is sprightly, various, and pleasant. The subject is of that kind which Gay was by nature qualified to adorn, yet some of his decorations may be justly wished away. An honest blacksmith might have done for Patty what is performed by Vulcan. The appearance of Cloacina is nauseous and superfluous; a shoe-boy could have been produced by the casual cohabitation of mere mortals. Horace's rule is broken in both cases; there is no dignus vindice nodus, no difficulty that required any supernatural interposition. A patten may be made by the hammer of a mortal, and a bastard may be dropped by a human strumpet. On great occasions, and on small, the mind is repelled by useless and apparent falsehood.

Of his little poems the public judgment seems to be right; they are neither much esteemed nor totally despised. The story of "The Apparition" is borrowed from one of the tales of Poggio. Those that please least are the pieces to which Gulliver gave occasion, for who can much delight in the echo of an unnatural fiction?

"Dione" is a counterpart to "Amynta" and "Pastor Fido" and other trifles of the same kind, easily imitated, and unworthy of imitation. What the Italians call comedies from a happy conclusion, Gay calls a tragedy from a mournful event, but the style of the Italians and of Gay is equally tragical. There is something in the poetical Arcadia so remote from known reality and speculative possibility that we can never support its representation through a long work. A pastoral of an hundred lines may be endured, but who will hear of sheep and goats, and myrtle bowers and purling rivulets, through five acts? Such scenes please barbarians in the dawn of literature, and children in the dawn of life, but will be for the most part thrown away as men grow wise and nations grow learned.

TICKELL.

Thomas Tickell, the son of the Rev. Richard Tickell, was born in 1686, at Bridekirk, in Cumberland, and in 1701 became a member of Queen's College in Oxford; in 1708 he was made Master of Arts, and two years afterwards was chosen Fellow, for which, as he did not comply with the statutes by taking orders, he obtained a dispensation from the Crown. He held his fellowship till 1726, and then vacated it by marrying, in that year, at Dublin.

Tickell was not one of those scholars who wear away their lives in closets; he entered early into the world and was long busy in public affairs, in which he was initiated under the patronage of Addison, whose notice he is said to have gained by his verses in praise of Rosamond. To those verses it would not have been just to deny regard, for they contain some of the most elegant encomiastic strains; and among the innumerable poems of the same kind it will be hard to find one with which they need to fear a comparison. It may deserve observation that when Pope wrote long afterwards in praise of Addison, he has copied—at least, has resembled—Tickell.

"Let joy salute fair Rosamonda's shade,
And wreaths of myrtle crown the lovely maid.
While now perhaps with Dido's ghost she roves,
And hears and tells the story of their loves,
Alike they mourn, alike they bless their fate,

Since Love, which made them wretched, made them great.
Nor longer that relentless doom bemoan,
Which gained a Virgil and an Addison."—TICKELL.

   "Then future ages with delight shall see
How Plato's, Bacon's, Newton's, looks agree;
Or in fair series laurelled bards be shown,
A Virgil there, and here an Addison."—POPE.

He produced another piece of the same kind at the appearance of Cato, with equal skill, but not equal happiness.

When the Ministers of Queen Anne were negotiating with France, Tickell published "The Prospect of Peace," a poem of which the tendency was to reclaim the nation from the pride of conquest to the pleasures of tranquillity. How far Tickell, whom Swift afterwards mentioned as Whiggissimus, had then connected himself with any party, I know not; this poem certainly did not flatter the practices, or promote the opinions, of the men by whom he was afterwards befriended.

Mr. Addison, however he hated the men then in power, suffered his friendship to prevail over his public spirit, and gave in the Spectator such praises of Tickell's poem that when, after having long wished to peruse it, I laid hold of it at last, I thought it unequal to the honours which it had received, and found it a piece to be approved rather than admired. But the hope excited by a work of genius, being general and indefinite, is rarely gratified. It was read at that with so much favour that six editions were sold.

At the arrival of King George, he sang "The Royal Progress," which, being inserted in the Spectator, is well known, and of which it is just to say that it is neither high nor low.

The poetical incident of most importance in Tickell's life was his publication of the first book of the "Iliad," as translated by himself, an apparent opposition to Pope's "Homer," of which the first part made its entrance into the world at the same time. Addison declared that the rival versions were both good, but that Tickell's was the best that ever was made; and with Addison, the wits, his adherents and followers, were certain to concur. Pope does not appear to have been much dismayed, "for," says he, "I have the town—that is, the mob—on my side." But he remarks "that it is common for the smaller party to make up in diligence what they want in numbers. He appeals to the people as his proper judges, and if they are not inclined to condemn him, he is in little care about the highflyers at Button's."

Pope did not long think Addison an impartial judge, for he considered him as the writer of Tickell's version. The reasons for his suspicion I will literally transcribe from Mr. Spence's Collection:—

"There had been a coldness," said Mr. Pope, "between Mr. Addison and me for some time, and we had not been in company together, for a good while, anywhere but at Button's Coffee House, where I used to see him almost every day. On his meeting me there, one day in particular, he took me aside and said he should be glad to dine with me at such a tavern, if I stayed till those people were gone (Budgell and Philips). He went accordingly, and after dinner Mr. Addison said 'that he had wanted for some time to talk with me: that his friend Tickell had formerly, whilst at Oxford, translated the first book of the Iliad; that he designed to print it, and had desired him to look it over; that he must therefore beg that I would not desire him to look over my first book, because, if he did, it would have the air of double-dealing.' I assured him that I did not at all take it ill of Mr. Tickell that he was going to publish his translation; that he certainly had as much right to translate any author as myself; and that publishing both was entering on a fair stage. I then added that I would not desire him to look over my first book of the Iliad, because he had looked over Mr. Tickell's, but could wish to have the benefit of his observations on my second, which I had then finished, and which Mr. Tickell had not touched upon. Accordingly I sent him the second book the next morning, and Mr. Addison a few days after returned it, with very high commendations. Soon after it was generally known that Mr. Tickell was publishing the first book of the Iliad, I met Dr. Young in the street, and upon our falling into that subject, the doctor expressed a great deal of surprise at Tickell's having had such a translation so long by him. He said that it was inconceivable to him, and that there must be some mistake in the matter; that each used to communicate to the other whatever verses they wrote, even to the least things; that Tickell could not have been busied in so long a work there without his knowing something of the matter; and that he had never heard a single word of it till on this occasion. This surprise of Dr. Young, together with what Steele has said against Tickell in relation to this affair, make it highly probable that there was some underhand dealing in that business; and indeed Tickell himself, who is a very fair worthy man, has since, in a manner, as good as owned it to me. When it was introduced into a conversation between Mr. Tickell and Mr. Pope by a third person, Tickell did not deny it, which, considering his honour and zeal for his departed friend, was the same as owning it."

Upon these suspicions, with which Dr. Warburton hints that other circumstances concurred, Pope always in his "Art of Sinking" quotes this book as the work of Addison.

To compare the two translations would be tedious; the palm is now given universally to Pope, but I think the first lines of Tickell's were rather to be preferred; and Pope seems to have since borrowed something from them in the correction of his own.

When the Hanover succession was disputed, Tickell gave what assistance his pen would supply. His "Letter to Avignon" stands high among party poems; it expresses contempt without coarseness, and superiority without insolence. It had the success which it deserved, being five times printed.

He was now intimately united to Mr. Addison, who, when he went into Ireland as secretary to the Lord Sunderland, took him thither, and employed him in public business; and when (1717) afterwards he rose to be Secretary of State, made him Under–Secretary. Their friendship seems to have continued without abatement; for, when Addison died, he left him the charge of publishing his works, with a solemn recommendation to the patronage of Craggs. To these works he prefixed an elegy on the author, which could owe none of its beauties to the assistance which might be suspected to have strengthened or embellished his earlier compositions; but neither he nor Addison ever produced nobler lines than are contained in the third and fourth paragraphs; nor is a more elegant funeral poem to be found in the whole compass of English literature. He was afterwards (about 1725) made secretary to the Lords Justices of Ireland, a place of great honour; in which he continued till 1740, when he died on the 23rd of April at Bath.

Of the poems yet unmentioned, the longest is "Kensington Gardens," of which the versification is smooth and elegant, but the fiction unskilfully compounded of Grecian deities and Gothic fairies. Neither species of those exploded beings could have done much; and when they are brought together, they only make each other contemptible. To Tickell, however, cannot be refused a high place among the minor poets; nor should it be forgotten that he was one of the contributors to the Spectator. With respect to his personal character, he is said to have been a man of gay conversation, at least a temperate lover of wine and company, and in his domestic relations without censure.

SOMERVILE.

Of Mr. Somervile's life I am not able to say anything that can satisfy curiosity. He was a gentleman whose estate lay in Warwickshire; his house, where he was born in 1693, is called Edston, a seat inherited from a long line of ancestors; for he was said to be of the first family in his county. He tells of himself that he was born near the Avon's banks. He was bred at Winchester school, and was elected fellow of New College. It does not appear that in the places of his education he exhibited any uncommon proofs of genius or literature. His powers were first displayed in the country, where he was distinguished as a poet, a gentleman, and a skilful and useful justice of the peace.

Of the close of his life, those whom his poems have delighted will read with pain the following account, copied from the "Letters" of his friend Shenstone, by whom he was too much resembled:—

"—Our old friend Somervile is dead! I did not imagine I could have been so sorry as I find myself on this occasion. Sublatum quaerimus. I can now excuse all his foibles; impute them to age, and to distress of circumstances: the last of these considerations wrings my very soul to think on. For a man of high spirit conscious of having (at least in one production) generally pleased the world, to be plagued and threatened by wretches that are low in every sense; to be forced to drink himself into pains of the body, in order to get rid of the pains of the mind is a misery."—He died July 19, 1742, and was buried at Wotton, near Henley on Arden.

His distresses need not be much pitied: his estate is said to be fifteen hundred a year, which by his death has devolved to Lord Somervile of Scotland. His mother. indeed, who lived till ninety, had a jointure of six hundred.

It is with regret that I find myself not better enabled to exhibit memorials of a writer who at least must be allowed to have set a good example to men of his own class, by devoting part of his time to elegant knowledge; and who has shown, by the subjects which his poetry has adorned, that it is practicable to be at once a skilful sportsman and a man of letters.

Somervile has tried many modes of poetry; and though perhaps he has not in any reached such excellence as to raise much envy, it may commonly be said at least, that "he writes very well for a gentleman." His serious pieces are sometimes elevated; and his trifles are sometimes elegant. In his verses to Addison, the couplet which mentions Clio is written with the most exquisite delicacy of praise; it exhibits one of those happy strokes that are seldom attained. In his Odes to Marlborough there are beautiful lines; but in the second Ode he shows that he knew little of his hero, when he talks of his private virtues. His subjects are commonly such as require no great depth of thought or energy of expression. His Fables are generally stale, and therefore excite no curiosity. Of his favourite, "The Two Springs," the fiction is unnatural, and the moral inconsequential. In his Tales there is too much coarseness, with too little care of language, and not sufficient rapidity of narration. His great work is his Chase, which he undertook in his maturer age, when his ear was improved to the approbation of blank verse, of which, however, his two first lines give a bad specimen. To this poem praise cannot be totally denied. He is allowed by sportsmen to write with great intelligence of his subject, which is the first requisite to excellence; and though it is impossible to interest the common readers of verse in the dangers or pleasures of the chase, he has done all that transition and variety could easily effect; and has with great propriety enlarged his plan by the modes of hunting used in other countries.

With still less judgment did he choose blank verse as the vehicle of "Rural Sports." If blank verse be not tumid and gorgeous, it is crippled prose; and familiar images in laboured language have nothing to recommend them but absurd novelty, which, wanting the attractions of nature, cannot please long. One excellence of the "Splendid Shilling" is, that it is short. Disguise can gratify no longer than it deceives.

THOMSON.

James Thomson, the son of a minister well esteemed for his piety and diligence, was born September 7, 1700, at Ednam, in the shire of Roxburgh, of which his father was pastor. His mother, whose name was Hume, inherited as co-heiress a portion of a small estate. The revenue of a parish in Scotland is seldom large; and it was probably in commiseration of the difficulty with which Mr. Thomson supported his family, having nine children, that Mr. Riccarton, a neighbouring minister, discovering in James uncommon promises of future excellence, undertook to superintend his education, and provide him books. He was taught the common rudiments of learning at the school of

Jedburgh, a place which he delights to recollect in his poem of "Autumn;" but was not considered by his master as superior to common boys, though in those early days he amused his patron and his friends with poetical compositions; with which, however, he so little pleased himself that on every New Year's Day he threw into the fire all the productions of the foregoing year.

From the school he was removed to Edinburgh, where he had not resided two years when his father died, and left all his children to the care of their mother, who raised upon her little estate what money a mortgage could afford; and, removing with her family to Edinburgh, lived to see her son rising into eminence.

The design of Thomson's friends was to breed him a minister. He lived at Edinburgh, at a school, without distinction or expectation, till at the usual time he performed a probationary exercise by explaining a psalm. His diction was so poetically splendid, that Mr. Hamilton, the professor of divinity, reproved him for speaking language unintelligible to a popular audience; and he censured one of his expressions as indecent, if not profane. This rebuke is reported to have repressed his thoughts of an ecclesiastical character, and he probably cultivated with new diligence his blossoms of poetry, which, however, were in some danger of a blast; for, submitting his productions to some who thought themselves qualified to criticise, he heard of nothing but faults; but, finding other judges more favourable, he did not suffer himself to sink into despondence. He easily discovered that the only stage on which a poet could appear with any hope of advantage was London; a place too wide for the operation of petty competition and private malignity, where merit might soon become conspicuous, and would find friends as soon as it became reputable to befriend it. A lady who was acquainted with his mother advised him to the journey, and promised some countenance or assistance, which at last he never received; however, he justified his adventure by her encouragement, and came to seek in London patronage and fame. At his arrival he found his way to Mr. Mallet, then tutor to the sons of the Duke of Montrose. He had recommendations to several persons of consequence, which he had tied up carefully in his handkerchief; but as he passed along the street, with the gaping curiosity of a newcomer, his attention was upon everything rather than his pocket, and his magazine of credentials was stolen from him.

His first want was a pair of shoes. For the supply of all his necessities, his whole fund was his "Winter," which for a time could find no purchaser; till at last Mr. Millan was persuaded to buy it at a low price; and this low price he had for some time reason to regret; but, by accident, Mr. Whately, a man not wholly unknown among authors, happening to turn his eye upon it, was so delighted that he ran from place to place celebrating its excellence. Thomson obtained likewise the notice of Aaron Hill, whom, being friendless and indigent, and glad of kindness, he courted with every expression of servile adulation.

"Winter" was dedicated to Sir Spencer Compton, but attracted no regard from him to the author; till Aaron Hill awakened his attention by some verses addressed to Thomson, and published in one of the newspapers, which censured the great for their neglect of ingenious men. Thomson then received a present of twenty guineas, of which he gives this account to Mr. Hill:—

I hinted to you in my last that on Saturday morning I was with Sir Spencer Compton. A certain gentleman, without my desire, spoke to him concerning me: his answer was that I had never come near him. Then the gentleman put the question, if he desired that I should wait on him? He returned, he did. On this the gentleman gave me an introductory letter to him. He received me in what they commonly call a civil manner; asked me some common−place questions, and made me a present of twenty guineas. I am very ready to own that the present was larger than my performance deserved; and shall ascribe it to his generosity, or any other cause, rather than the merit of the address."

The poem, which, being of a new kind, few would venture at first to like, by degrees gained upon the public; and one edition was very speedily succeeded by another.

Thomson's credit was now high, and every day brought him new friends; among others Dr. Rundle, a man afterwards unfortunately famous, sought his acquaintance, and found his qualities such that he recommended him to the Lord Chancellor Talbot.

"Winter" was accompanied, in many editions, not only with a preface and dedication, but with poetical praises by Mr. Hill, Mr. Mallet (then Malloch), and Mira, the fictitious name of a lady once too well known. Why the dedications are, to "Winter" and the other Seasons, contrarily to custom, left out in the collected works, the reader may inquire.

The next year (1727) he distinguished himself by three publications: of "Summer," in pursuance of his plan; of "A Poem on the Death of Sir Isaac Newton," which he was enabled to perform as an exact philosopher by the instruction of Mr. Gray; and of

"Britannia," a kind of poetical invective against the Ministry, whom the nation then thought not forward enough in resenting the depredations of the Spaniards. By this piece he declared himself an adherent to the Opposition, and had therefore no favour to expect from the Court.

Thomson, having been some time entertained in the family of Lord Binning, was desirous of testifying his gratitude by making him the patron of his "Summer;" but the same kindness which had first disposed Lord Binning to encourage him, determined him to refuse the dedication, which was by his advice addressed to Mr. Dodington, a man who had more power to advance the reputation and fortune of a poet.

"Spring" was published next year, with a dedication to the Countess of Hertford, whose practice it was to invite every summer some poet into the country, to hear her verses and assist her studies. This honour was one summer conferred on Thomson, who took more delight in carousing with Lord Hertford and his friends than assisting her ladyship's poetical operations, and therefore never received another summons.

"Autumn," the season to which the "Spring" and "Summer" are preparatory, still remained unsung, and was delayed till he published (1730) his works collected.

He produced in 1727 the tragedy of Sophonisba, which raised such expectation that every rehearsal was dignified with a splendid audience, collected to anticipate the delight that was preparing for the public. It was observed, however, that nobody was much affected, and that the company rose as from a moral lecture. It had upon the stage no unusual degree of success. Slight accidents will operate upon the taste of pleasure. There is a feeble line in the play:—

"O Sophonisba, Sophonisba, O!"

This gave occasion to a waggish parody—

"O, Jemmy Thomson, Jemmy Thomson, O!"

which for a while was echoed through the town.

I have been told by Savage, that of the prologue to Sophonisba, the first part was written by Pope, who could not be persuaded to finish it; and that the concluding lines were added by Mallet.

Thomson was not long afterwards, by the influence of Dr. Rundle, sent to travel with Mr. Charles Talbot, the eldest son of the Chancellor. He was yet young enough to receive new impressions, to have his opinions rectified and his views enlarged; nor can he be supposed to have wanted that curiosity which is inseparable from an active and comprehensive mind. He may therefore now be supposed to have revelled in all the joys of intellectual luxury; he was every day feasted with instructive novelties; he lived splendidly without expense: and might expect when he returned home a certain establishment.

At this time a long course of opposition to Sir Robert Walpole had filled the nation with clamours for liberty, of which no man felt the want, and with care for liberty which was not in danger. Thomson, in his travels on the Continent, found or fancied so many evils arising from the tyranny of other governments, that he resolved to write a very long poem, in five parts, upon Liberty. While he was busy on the first book, Mr. Talbot died; and Thomson, who had been rewarded for his attendance by the place of secretary of the briefs, pays in the initial lines a decent tribute to his memory. Upon this great poem two years were spent, and the author congratulated himself upon it as his noblest work; but an author and his reader are not always of a mind. Liberty called in vain upon her votaries to read her praises, and reward her encomiast: her praises were condemned to harbour spiders, and to gather dust: none of Thomson's performances were so little regarded. The judgment of the public was not erroneous; the recurrence of the same images must tire in time; an enumeration of examples to prove a position which nobody denied, as it was from the beginning superfluous, must quickly grow disgusting.

The poem of "Liberty" does not now appear in its original state; but, when the author's works were collected after his death, was shortened by Sir George Lyttelton, with a liberty which, as it has a manifest tendency to lessen the confidence of society, and to confound the characters of authors, by making one man write by the judgment of another, cannot be justified by any supposed propriety of the alteration, or kindness of the friend. I wish to see it exhibited as its author left it.

Thomson now lived in ease and plenty, and seems for a while to have suspended his poetry: but he was soon called back to labour by the death of the Chancellor, for his place then became vacant; and though the Lord Hardwicke delayed for some time to give it away, Thomson's bashfulness or pride, or some other motive perhaps not more laudable, withheld him from soliciting; and the new Chancellor would not give him what he would not ask. He now relapsed to his former indigence; but the Prince of Wales was at that time struggling for popularity, and by the influence of Mr. Lyttelton professed himself the patron of wit; to him Thomson was introduced, and being gaily interrogated about the state of his affairs said "that they were in a more poetical posture than formerly," and had a pension allowed him of one hundred pounds a year.

Being now obliged to write, he produced (1738) the tragedy of Agamemnon, which was much shortened in the representation. It had the fate which most commonly attends mythological stories, and was only endured, but not favoured. It struggled with such difficulty through the first night that Thomson, coming late to his friends with whom he was to sup, excused his delay by telling them how the sweat of his distress had so disordered his wig that he could not come till he had been refitted by a barber. He so interested himself in his own drama that, if I remember right, as he sat in the upper gallery, he accompanied the players by audible recitation, till a friendly hint frighted him to silence. Pope countenanced Agamemnon by coming to it, the first night, and was welcomed to the theatre by a general clap; he had much regard for Thomson, and once expressed it in a poetical epistle sent to Italy, of which, however, he abated the value by transplanting some of the lines into his Epistle to Arbuthnot.

About this time (1737) the Act was passed for licensing plays, of which the first operation was the prohibition of Gustavus Vasa, a tragedy of Mr. Brooke, whom the public recompensed by a very liberal subscription; the next was the refusal of Edward and Eleonora, offered by Thomson. It is hard to discover why either play should have been obstructed. Thomson likewise endeavoured to repair his loss by a subscription, of which I cannot now tell the success. When the public murmured at the unkind treatment of Thomson, one of the Ministerial writers remarked that "he had taken a Liberty which was not agreeable to Britannia in any Season." He was soon after employed, in conjunction with Mr. Mallet, to write the masque of Alfred, which was acted before the Prince at Cliefden House.

His next work (1745) was, Tancred and Sigismunda, the most successful of all his tragedies, for it still keeps its turn upon the stage. It may be doubted whether he was, either by the bent of nature or habits of study, much qualified for tragedy. It does not appear that he had much sense of the pathetic; and his diffusive and descriptive style produced declamation rather than dialogue. His friend Mr. Lyttelton was now in power, and conferred upon him the office of Surveyor–General of the Leeward Islands; from which, when his deputy was paid, he received about three hundred pounds a year.

The last piece that he lived to publish was the "Castle of Indolence," which was many years under his hand, but was at last finished with great accuracy. The first canto opens a scene of lazy luxury that fills the imagination. He was now at ease, but was not long to enjoy it, for, by taking cold on the water between London and Kew, he caught a disorder, which, with some careless exasperation, ended in a fever that put an end to his life, August 27, 1748. He was buried in the church of Richmond, without an inscription; but a monument has been erected to his memory in Westminster Abbey.

Thomson was of stature above the middle size, and "more fat than bard beseems," of a dull countenance and a gross, unanimated, uninviting appearance; silent in mingled company, but cheerful among select friends, and by his friends very tenderly and warmly beloved. He left behind him the tragedy of Coriolanus, which was, by the zeal of his patron, Sir George Lyttelton, brought upon the stage for the benefit of his family, and recommended by a prologue, which Quin, who had long lived with Thomson in fond intimacy, spoke in such a manner as showed him "to be," on that occasion, "no actor." The commencement of this benevolence is very honourable to Quin, who is reported to have delivered Thomson, then known to him only for his genius, from an arrest by a very considerable present; and its continuance is honourable to both, for friendship is not always the sequel of obligation. By this tragedy a considerable sum was raised, of which part discharged his debts, and the rest was remitted to his sisters, whom, however removed from them by place or condition, he regarded with great tenderness, as will appear by the following letter, which I communicate with much pleasure, as it gives me at once an opportunity of recording the fraternal kindness of Thomson, and reflecting on the friendly assistance of Mr. Boswell, from whom I received it:—

"Hagley in Worcestershire, October the 4th, 1747.

"My Dear Sister,—I thought you had known me better than to interpret my silence into a decay of affection, especially as your behaviour has always been such as rather to increase than diminish it. Don't imagine, because I am a bad correspondent, that I can ever prove an unkind friend and brother. I must do myself the justice to tell you that my affections are naturally very fixed and constant; and if I had ever reason of complaint against you (of which, by–the–bye, I have not the least shadow), I am conscious of so many defects in myself as dispose me to be not a little charitable and forgiving.

"It gives me the truest heart–felt satisfaction to hear you have a good kind husband, and are in easy contented circumstances; but were they otherwise, that would only awaken and heighten my tenderness towards you. As our good and tender–hearted parents did not live to receive any material testimonies of that highest human gratitude I owed them (than which nothing could have given me equal pleasure), the only return I can make them now is by kindness to those they left behind them. Would to God poor Lizy had lived longer, to have been a farther witness of the truth of what I say and that I might have had the pleasure of seeing once more a sister who so truly deserved my esteem and love! But she is happy, while we must toil a little longer here below: let us, however, do it cheerfully and gratefully, supported by the pleasing hope of meeting you again on a safer shore, where to recollect the storms and difficulties of life will not perhaps be inconsistent with that blissful state. You did right to call your daughter by her name: for you must needs have had a particular tender friendship for one another, endeared as you were by nature, by having passed the affectionate years of your youth together: and by that great softener and engager of hearts, mutual hardship. That it was in my power to ease it a little, I account one of the most exquisite pleasures of my life. But enough of this melancholy, though not unpleasing, strain.

"I esteem you for your sensible and disinterested advice to Mr. Bell, as you will see by my letter to him. As I approve entirely of his marrying again, you may readily ask me why I don't marry at all. My circumstances have hitherto been so variable and uncertain in this fluctuating world, as induce to keep me from engaging in such a state: and now, though they are more settled, and of late (which you will be glad to hear) considerably improved, I begin to think myself too far advanced in life for such youthful undertakings, not to mention some other petty reasons that are apt to startle the delicacy of difficult old bachelors. I am, however, not a little suspicious that, was I to pay a visit to Scotland (which I have some thought of doing soon), I might possibly be tempted to think of a thing not easily repaired if done amiss. I have always been of opinion that none make better wives than the ladies of Scotland; and yet who more forsaken than they, while the gentlemen are continually running abroad all the world over? Some of them, it is true, are wise enough to return for a wife. You see, I am beginning to make interest already with the Scots ladies. But no more of this infectious subject. Pray let me hear from you now and then; and though I am not a regular correspondent, yet perhaps I may mend in that respect. Remember me kindly to your husband, and believe me to be

> "Your most affectionate Brother,
> "James Thomson." (Addressed) "To Mrs. Thomson in Lanark."

The benevolence of Thomson was fervid, but not active; he would give on all occasions what assistance his purse would supply, but the offices of intervention or solicitation he could not conquer his sluggishness sufficiently to perform. The affairs of others, however, were not more neglected than his own. He had often felt the inconveniences of idleness, but he never cured it; and was so conscious of his own character that he talked of writing an Eastern tale "Of the Man who Loved to be in Distress." Among his peculiarities was a very unskilful and inarticulate manner of pronouncing any lofty or solemn composition. He was once reading to Dodington, who, being himself a reader eminently elegant, was so much provoked by his odd utterance that he snatched the paper from his hands and told him that he did not understand his own verses.

The biographer of Thomson has remarked that an author's life is best read in his works; his observation was not well timed. Savage, who lived much with Thomson, once told me how he heard a lady remarking that she could gather from his works three−parts of his character: that he was "a great lover, a great swimmer, and rigorously abstinent;" "but," said Savage, "he knows not any love but that of the sex; he was, perhaps, never in cold water in his life; and he indulges himself in all the luxury that comes within his reach." Yet Savage always spoke with the most eager praise of his social qualities, his warmth and constancy of friendship, and his adherence to his first acquaintance when the advancement of his reputation had left them behind him.

As a writer, he is entitled to one praise of the highest kind: his mode of thinking and of expressing his thoughts is original. His blank verse is no more the blank verse of Milton, or of any other poet, than the rhymes of Prior are the rhymes of Cowley. His numbers, his pauses, his diction, are of his own growth, without transcription, without imitation. He thinks in a peculiar train, and he thinks always as a man of genius; he looks round on

Nature and on Life with the eye which Nature bestows only on a poet; the eye that distinguishes in everything presented to its view whatever there is on which imagination can delight to be detained, and with a mind that at once comprehends the vast and attends to the minute. The reader of the "Seasons" wonders that he never saw before what Thomson shows him, and that he never yet has felt what Thomson impresses. His is one of the works in which blank verse seems properly used. Thomson's wide expansion of general views, and his enumeration of circumstantial varieties, would have been obstructed and embarrassed by the frequent intersections of the sense, which are the necessary effects of rhyme. His descriptions of extended scenes and general effects bring before us the whole magnificence of Nature, whether pleasing or dreadful. The gaiety of Spring, the splendour of Summer, the tranquillity of Autumn, and the horror of Winter, take in their turns possession of the mind. The poet leads us through the appearances of things as they are successively varied by the vicissitudes of the year, and imparts to us so much of his own enthusiasm that our thoughts expand with his imagery and kindle with his sentiments. Nor is the naturalist without his part in the entertainment, for he is assisted to recollect and to combine, to arrange his discoveries, and to amplify the sphere of his contemplation. The great defect of the "Seasons" is want of method; but for this I know not that there was any remedy. Of many appearances subsisting all at once, no rule can be given why one should be mentioned before another; yet the memory wants the help of order, and the curiosity is not excited by suspense or expectation. His diction is in the highest degree florid and luxuriant, such as may be said to be to his images and thoughts "both their lustre and their shade;" such as invests them with splendour, through which, perhaps, they are not always easily discerned. It is too exuberant, and sometimes may be charged with filling the ear more than the mind.

These poems, with which I was acquainted at their first appearance, I have since found altered and enlarged by subsequent revisals, as the author supposed his judgment to grow more exact, and as books or conversation extended his knowledge and opened his prospects. They are, I think, improved in general; yet I know not whether they have not lost part of what Temple calls their "race," a word which, applied to wines in its primitive sense, means the flavour of the soil.

"Liberty," when it first appeared, I tried to read, and soon desisted. I have never tried again, and therefore will not hazard either praise or censure. The highest praise which he has received ought not to be suppressed: it is said by Lord Lyttelton, in the Prologue to his posthumous play, that his works contained

"No line which, dying, he could wish to blot."

WATTS.

The poems of Dr. Watts were, by my recommendation, inserted in the late Collection, the readers of which are to impute to me whatever pleasure or weariness they may find in the perusal of Blackmore, Watts, Pomfret, and Yalden.

Isaac Watts was born July 17, 1674, at Southampton, where his father, of the same name, kept a boarding-school for young gentlemen, though common report makes him a shoemaker. He appears, from the narrative of Dr. Gibbons, to have been neither indigent nor illiterate.

Isaac, the eldest of nine children, was given to books from his infancy, and began, we are told, to learn Latin when he was four years old—I suppose, at home. He was afterwards taught Latin, Greek, and Hebrew, by Mr. Pinhorne, a clergyman, master of the Free School at Southampton, to whom the gratitude of his scholar afterwards inscribed a Latin ode. His proficiency at school was so conspicuous that a subscription was proposed for his support at the University, but he declared his resolution of taking his lot with the Dissenters. Such he was as every Christian Church would rejoice to have adopted. He therefore repaired, in 1690, to an academy taught by Mr. Rowe, where he had for his companions and fellow students Mr. Hughes the poet, and Dr. Horte, afterwards Archbishop of Tuam. Some Latin Essays, supposed to have been written as exercises at this academy, show a degree of knowledge, both philosophical and theological, such as very few attain by a much longer course of study. He was, as he hints in his "Miscellanies," a maker of verses from fifteen to fifty, and in his youth he appears to have paid attention to Latin poetry. His verses to his brother, in the glyconic measure, written when he was seventeen, are remarkably easy and elegant. Some of his other odes are deformed by the Pindaric folly then prevailing, and are written with such neglect of all metrical rules as is without example among the ancients; but his diction, though perhaps not always exactly pure, has such copiousness and splendour as shows that he was but a very little distance from excellence. His method of study was to impress the contents of his books upon his memory by abridging them, and by interleaving them to amplify one system with supplements from another.

With the congregation of his tutor, Mr. Rowe, who were, I believe, Independents, he communicated in his nineteenth year. At the age of twenty he left the academy, and spent two years in study and devotion at the house of his father, who treated him with great tenderness, and had the happiness, indulged to few parents, of living to see his son eminent for literature and venerable for piety. He was then entertained by Sir John Hartopp five years, as domestic tutor to his son, and in that time particularly devoted himself to the study of the Holy Scriptures; and, being chosen assistant to Dr. Chauncey, preached the first time on the birthday that completed his twenty–fourth year, probably considering that as the day of a second nativity, by which he entered on a new period of existence.

In about three years he succeeded Dr. Chauncey; but soon after his entrance on his charge he was seized by a dangerous illness, which sunk him to such weakness that the congregation thought an assistant necessary, and appointed Mr. Price. His health then returned gradually, and he performed his duty till (1712) he was seized by a fever of such violence and continuance, that from the feebleness which it brought upon him he never perfectly recovered. This calamitous state made the compassion of his friends necessary, and drew upon him the attention of Sir Thomas Abney, who received him into his house, where, with a constancy of friendship and uniformity of conduct not often to be found, he was treated for thirty–six years with all the kindness that friendship could prompt, and all the attention that respect could dictate. Sir Thomas died about eight years afterwards, but he continued with the lady and her daughters to the end of his life. The lady died about a year after him.

A coalition like this, a state in which the notions of patronage and dependence were overpowered by the perception of reciprocal benefits, deserves a particular memorial; and I will not withhold from the reader Dr. Gibbons's representation, to which regard is to be paid as to the narrative of one who writes what he knows, and what is known likewise to multitudes besides:—

"Our next observation shall be made upon that remarkably kind Providence which brought the Doctor into Sir Thomas Abney's family, and continued him there till his death, a period of no less than thirty–six years. In the midst of his sacred labours for the glory of God, and good of his generation, he is seized with a most violent and threatening fever, which leaves him oppressed with great weakness, and puts a stop at least to his public services for four years. In this distressing season, doubly so to his active and pious spirit, he is invited to Sir Thomas Abney's family, nor ever removes from it till he had finished his days. Here he enjoyed the uninterrupted demonstrations of the truest friendship. Here, without any care of his own, he had everything which could contribute to the enjoyment of life, and favour the unwearied pursuit of his studies. Here he dwelt in a family which, for piety, order, harmony, and every virtue, was a house of God. Here he had the privilege of a country recess, the fragrant bower, the spreading lawn, the flowery garden, and other advantages, to soothe his mind and aid his restoration to health; to yield him, whenever he chose them, most grateful intervals from his laborious studies, and enable him to return to them with redoubled vigour and delight. Had it not been for this most happy event, he might, as to outward view, have feebly, it may be painfully, dragged on through many more years of languor, and inability for public service, and even for profitable study, or perhaps might have sunk into his grave under the overwhelming load of infirmities in the midst of his days; and thus the Church and world would have been deprived of those many excellent sermons and works which he drew up and published during his long residence in this family. In a few years after his coming hither, Sir Thomas Abney dies; but his amiable consort survives, who shows the Doctor the same respect and friendship as before, and most happily for him and great numbers besides; for, as her riches were great, her generosity and munificence were in full proportion; her thread of life was drawn out to a great age, even beyond that of the Doctor's, and thus this excellent man, through her kindness, and that of her daughter, the present Mrs. Elizabeth Abney, who in a like degree esteemed and honoured him, enjoyed all the benefits and felicities he experienced at his first entrance into this family till his days were numbered and finished, and, like a shock of corn in its season, he ascended into the regions of perfect and immortal life and joy."

If this quotation has appeared long, let it be considered that it comprises an account of six–and–thirty years, and those the years of Dr. Watts.

From the time of his reception into this family his life was no otherwise diversified than by successive publications. The series of his works I am not able to deduce; their number and their variety show the intenseness of his industry and the extent of his capacity. He was one of the first authors that taught the Dissenters to court attention by the graces of language. Whatever they had among them before, whether of learning or acuteness, was commonly obscured and blunted by coarseness and inelegance of style. He showed them that zeal and purity might be expressed and enforced by polished diction. He continued to the end of his life a teacher of a congregation, and no reader of his works can doubt his fidelity or diligence. In the pulpit, though his low stature, which very little exceeded five feet, graced him with no advantages of appearance, yet the gravity and propriety of his utterance made his discourses very efficacious. I once mentioned the reputation which Mr. Foster had gained by his proper delivery, to my friend Dr. Hawkesworth, who told me that in the art of pronunciation he was far inferior to Dr. Watts. Such was his flow of thoughts, and such his promptitude of language, that in the latter part of his life he did not precompose his cursory sermons, but, having adjusted the heads and sketched out some particulars, trusted for success to his extemporary powers. He did not endeavour to assist his eloquence by any gesticulations; for, as no corporeal actions have any correspondence with theological truth, he did not see how they could enforce it. At the conclusion of weighty sentences he gave time, by a short pause, for the proper impression.

To stated and public instruction he added familiar visits and personal application, and was careful to improve the opportunities which conversation offered of diffusing and increasing the influence of religion. By his natural temper he was quick of resentment; but by his established and habitual practice he was gentle, modest, and inoffensive. His tenderness appeared in his attention to children, and to the poor. To the poor, while he lived in the family of his friend, he allowed the third part of his annual revenue; though the whole was not a hundred a year; and for children he condescended to lay aside the scholar, the philosopher, and the wit, to write little poems of devotion, and systems of instruction, adapted to their wants and capacities, from the dawn of reason through its gradations of advance in the morning of life. Every man acquainted with the common principles of human action will look with veneration on the writer who is at one time combating Locke, and at another making a catechism for children in their fourth year. A voluntary descent from the dignity of science is perhaps the hardest lesson that humility can teach.

As his mind was capacious, his curiosity excursive, and his industry continual, his writings are very numerous and his subjects various. With his theological works I am only enough acquainted to admire his meekness of opposition, and his mildness of censure. It was not only in his book, but in his mind, that orthodoxy was united with charity.

Of his philosophical pieces, his "Logic" has been received into the Universities, and therefore wants no private recommendation; if he owes part of it to Le Clerc, it must be considered that no man who undertakes merely to methodise or illustrate a system pretends to be its author.

In his metaphysical disquisitions it was observed by the late learned Mr. Dyer, that he confounded the idea of SPACE with that of EMPTY SPACE, and did not consider that though space might be without matter, yet matter being extended could not be without space.

Few books have been perused by me with greater pleasure than his "Improvement of the Mind," of which the radical principle may indeed be found in Locke's "Conduct of the Understanding;" but they are so expanded and ramified by Watts, as to confer upon him the merit of a work in the highest degree useful and pleasing. Whoever has the care of instructing others may be charged with deficiency in his duty if this book is not recommended.

I have mentioned his treatises of theology as distinct from his other productions; but the truth is that whatever he took in hand was, by his incessant solicitude for souls, converted to theology. As piety predominated in his mind, it is diffused over his works. Under his direction it may be truly said, Theologiae philosophia ancillatur (Philosophy is subservient to evangelical instruction). It is difficult to read a page without learning, or at least wishing, to be better. The attention is caught by indirect instruction; and he that sat down only to reason is on a sudden compelled to pray. It was therefore with great propriety that, in 1728, he received from Edinburgh and Aberdeen an unsolicited diploma, by which he became a Doctor of Divinity. Academical honours would have more value if they were always bestowed with equal judgment. He continued many years to study and to preach, and to do good by his instruction and example, till at last the infirmities of age disabled him from the more laborious part of his ministerial functions, and, being no longer capable of public duty, he offered to remit the salary appendent to it; but his congregation would not accept the resignation. By degrees his weakness increased, and at last confined him to his chamber and his bed, where he was worn gradually away without pain, till he expired November 25th 1748, in the seventy–fifth year of his age.

Few men have left behind such purity of character, or such monuments of laborious piety. He has provided instruction for all ages—from those who are lisping their first lessons, to the enlightened readers of Malebranche and Locke; he has left neither corporeal nor spiritual nature unexamined; he has taught the art of reasoning, and the science of the stars. His character, therefore, must be formed from the multiplicity and diversity of his attainments, rather than from any single performance, for it would not be safe to claim for him the highest rank in any single denomination of literary dignity; yet, perhaps, there was nothing in which he would not have excelled, if he had not divided his powers to different pursuits.

As a poet, had he been only a poet, he would probably have stood high among the authors with whom he is now associated. For his judgment was exact, and he noted beauties and faults with very nice discernment; his imagination, as the "Dacian Battle" proves, was vigorous and active, and the stores of knowledge were large by which his fancy was to be supplied. His ear was well tuned, and his diction was elegant and copious. But his devotional poetry is, like that of others, unsatisfactory. The paucity of its topics enforces perpetual repetition, and the sanctity of the matter rejects the ornaments of figurative diction. It is sufficient for Watts to have done better than others what no man has done well. His poems on other subjects seldom rise higher than might be expected from the amusements of a man of letters, and have different degrees of value as they are more or less laboured, or as the occasion was more or less favourable to invention. He writes too often without regular measures, and too often in blank verse; the rhymes are not always sufficiently correspondent. He is particularly unhappy in coining names expressive of characters. His lines are commonly smooth and easy, and his thoughts always religiously pure; but who is there that, to so much piety and innocence, does not wish for a greater measure of sprightliness and vigour? He is at least one of the few poets with whom youth and ignorance may be safely pleased; and happy will be that reader whose mind is disposed, by his verses or his prose, to imitate him in all but his non–conformity, to copy his benevolence to man, and his reverence to God.

A. PHILIPS.

Of the birth or early part of the life of Ambrose Philips I have not been able to find any account. His academical education he received at St. John's College in Cambridge, where he first solicited the notice of the world by some English verses, in the collection published by the University on the death of Queen Mary. From this time how he was employed, or in what station he passed his life, is not yet discovered. He must have published his "Pastorals" before the year 1708, because they are evidently prior to those of Pope. He afterwards (1709) addressed to the universal patron, the Duke of Dorset, a

"Poetical Letter from Copenhagen," which was published in the Tatler, and is by Pope, in one of his first Letters, mentioned with high praise as the production of a man "who could write very nobly."

Philips was a zealous Whig, and therefore easily found access to Addison and Steele; but his ardour seems not to have procured him anything more than kind words, since he was reduced to translate the "Persian Tales" for Tonson, for which he was afterwards reproached, with this addition of contempt, that he worked for half–a–crown. The book is divided into many sections, for each of which, if he received half–a–crown, his reward, as writers then were paid, was very liberal; but half–a–crown had a mean sound. He was employed in promoting the principles of his party, by epitomising Hacket's "Life of Archbishop Williams." The original book is written with such depravity of genius, such mixture of the fop and pedant, as has not often appeared. The epitome is free enough from affectation, but has little spirit or vigour.

In 1712 he brought upon the stage The Distressed Mother, almost a translation of Racine's Andromaque. Such a work requires no uncommon powers, but the friends of Philips exerted every art to promote his interest. Before the appearance of the play a whole Spectator, none indeed of the best, was devoted to its praise; while it yet continued to be acted, another Spectator was written to tell what impression it made upon Sir Roger, and on the first night a select audience, says Pope, was called together to applaud it. It was concluded with the most successful Epilogue that was ever yet spoken on the English theatre. The three first nights it was recited twice, and not only continued to be demanded through the run, as it is termed, of the play, but whenever it is recalled to the stage, where by peculiar fortune, though a copy from the French, it yet keeps its place, the Epilogue is still expected, and is still spoken.

The propriety of Epilogues in general, and consequently of this, was questioned by a correspondent of the Spectator, whose letter was undoubtedly admitted for the sake of the answer, which soon followed, written with much zeal and acrimony. The attack and the defence equally contributed to stimulate curiosity and continue attention. It may be discovered in the defence that Prior's Epilogue to Phaedra had a little excited jealousy, and something of Prior's plan may be discovered in the performance of his rival. Of this distinguished Epilogue the reputed author was the wretched Budgell, whom Addison used to denominate "the man who calls me cousin;" and when he was asked how such a silly fellow could write so well, replied, "The Epilogue was quite another thing when I saw it first." It was known in Tonson's family, and told to Garrick, that Addison was himself the author of it, and that, when it had been at first printed with his name, he came early in the morning, before the copies were distributed, and ordered it to be given to Budgell, that it might add weight to the solicitation which he was then making for a place.

Philips was now high in the ranks of literature. His play was applauded; his translations from Sappho had been published in the Spectator; he was an important and distinguished associate of clubs, witty and poetical; and nothing was wanting to his happiness but that he should be sure of its continuance. The work which had procured him the first notice from the public was his "Six Pastorals," which, flattering the imagination with Arcadian scenes, probably found many readers, and might have long passed as a pleasing amusement had they not been unhappily too much commended.

The rustic poems of Theocritus were so highly valued by the Greeks and Romans that they attracted the imitation of Virgil, whose Eclogues seem to have been considered as precluding all attempts of the same kind; for no shepherds were taught to sing by any succeeding poet, till Nemesian and Calphurnius ventured their feeble efforts in the lower age of Latin literature.

At the revival of learning in Italy it was soon discovered that a dialogue of imaginary swains might be composed with little difficulty, because the conversation of shepherds excludes profound or refined sentiment; and for images and descriptions, satyrs and fauns, and naiads and dryads, were always within call; and woods and meadows, and hills and rivers, supplied variety of matter, which, having a natural power to soothe the mind, did not quickly cloy it.

Petrarch entertained the learned men of his age with the novelty of modern pastorals in Latin. Being not ignorant of Greek, and finding nothing in the word "eclogue" of rural meaning, he supposed it to be corrupted by the copiers, and therefore called his own productions "AEglogues," by which he meant to express the talk of goat–herds, though it will mean only the talk of goats. This new name was adopted by subsequent writers, and among others by our Spenser.

More than a century afterwards (1498) Mantuan published his Bucolics with such success that they were soon dignified by Badius with a comment, and, as Scaliger complained, received into schools, and taught as classical; his complaint was vain, and the practice, however injudicious, spread far and continued long. Mantuan was read, at least in some of the inferior schools of this kingdom, to the beginning of the present century. The speakers of Mantuan carried their disquisitions beyond the country to censure the corruptions of the Church, and from him Spenser learned to employ his swains on topics of controversy. The Italians soon transferred pastoral poetry into their own language. Sannazaro wrote "Arcadia" in prose and verse; Tasso and Guarini wrote "Favole Boschareccie," or Sylvan Dramas; and all nations of Europe filled volumes with Thyrsis and Damon, and Thestylis and Phyllis.

Philips thinks it "somewhat strange to conceive how, in an age so addicted to the Muses, pastoral poetry never comes to be so much as thought upon." His wonder seems very unseasonable; there had never, from the time of Spenser, wanted writers to talk occasionally of Arcadia and Strephon, and half the book, in which he first tried his powers, consists of dialogues on Queen Mary's death, between Tityrus and Corydon, or Mopsus and Menalcas. A series or book of pastorals, however, I know not that anyone had then lately published.

Not long afterwards Pope made the first display of his powers in four pastorals, written in a very different form. Philips had taken Spenser, and Pope took Virgil for his pattern. Philips endeavoured to be natural, Pope laboured to be elegant.

Philips was now favoured by Addison and by Addison's companions, who were very willing to push him into reputation. The Guardian gave an account of Pastoral, partly critical and partly historical; in which, when the merit of the modern is compared, Tasso and Guarini are censured for remote thoughts and unnatural refinements, and, upon the whole, the Italians and French are all excluded from rural poetry, and the pipe of the pastoral muse is transmitted by lawful inheritance from Theocritus to Virgil, from Virgil to Spenser, and from Spenser to Philips. With this inauguration of Philips his rival Pope was not much delighted; he therefore drew a comparison of Philips's performance with his own, in which, with an unexampled and unequalled artifice of irony, though he has himself always the advantage, he gives the preference to Philips. The design of aggrandising himself he disguised with such dexterity that, though Addison discovered it, Steele was deceived, and was afraid of displeasing Pope by publishing his paper. Published however it was (Guardian, No. 40), and from that time Pope and Philips lived in a perpetual reciprocation of malevolence. In poetical powers, of either praise or satire, there was no proportion between the combatants; but Philips, though he could not prevail by wit, hoped to hurt Pope with another weapon, and charged him, as Pope thought with Addison's approbation, as disaffected to the Government. Even with this he was not satisfied, for, indeed, there is no appearance that any regard was paid to his clamours. He proceeded to grosser insults, and hung up a rod at Button's, with which he threatened to chastise Pope, who appears to have been extremely exasperated, for in the first edition of his Letters he calls Philips "rascal," and in the last still charges him with detaining in his hands the subscriptions for "Homer" delivered to him by the Hanover Club. I suppose it was never suspected that he meant to appropriate the money; he only delayed, and with sufficient meanness, the gratification of him by whose prosperity he was pained.

Men sometimes suffer by injudicious kindness; Philips became ridiculous, without his own fault, by the absurd admiration of his friends, who decorated him with honorary garlands, which the first breath of contradiction blasted.

When upon the succession of the House of Hanover every Whig expected to be happy, Philips seems to have obtained too little notice; he caught few drops of the golden shower, though he did not omit what flattery could perform. He was only made a commissioner of the lottery (1717), and, what did not much elevate his character, a justice of the peace.

The success of his first play must naturally dispose him to turn his hopes towards the stage; he did not, however, soon commit himself to the mercy of an audience, but contented himself with the fame already acquired, till after nine years he produced (1722) The Briton, a tragedy which, whatever was its reception, is now neglected; though one of the scenes, between Vanoc the British Prince and Valens the Roman General, is confessed to be written with great dramatic skill, animated by spirit truly poetical. He had not been idle though he had been silent, for he exhibited another tragedy the same year on the story of Humphry, Duke of Gloucester. This tragedy is only remembered by its title.

His happiest undertaking was (1711) of a paper called The Freethinker, in conjunction with associates, of whom one was Dr. Boulter, who, then only minister of a parish in Southwark, was of so much consequence to the Government that he was made first Bishop of Bristol, and afterwards Primate of Ireland, where his piety and his charity will be long honoured. It may easily be imagined that what was printed under the direction of Boulter would have nothing in it indecent or licentious; its title is to be understood as

Lives of the Poets

implying only freedom from unreasonable prejudice. It has been reprinted in volumes, but is little read; nor can impartial criticism recommend it as worthy of revival.

Boulter was not well qualified to write diurnal essays, but he knew how to practise the liberality of greatness and the fidelity of friendship. When he was advanced to the height of ecclesiastical dignity, he did not forget the companion of his labours. Knowing Philips to be slenderly supported, he took him to Ireland as partaker of his fortune, and, making him his secretary, added such preferments as enabled him to represent the county of Armagh in the Irish Parliament. In December, 1726, he was made secretary to the Lord Chancellor, and in August, 1733, became Judge of the Prerogative Court.

After the death of his patron he continued some years in Ireland, but at last longing, as it seems, for his native country, he returned (1748) to London, having doubtless survived most of his friends and enemies, and among them his dreaded antagonist Pope. He found, however, the Duke of Newcastle still living, and to him he dedicated his poems collected into a volume.

Having purchased an annuity of 400 pounds, he now certainly hoped to pass some years of life in plenty and tranquillity; but his hope deceived him: he was struck with a palsy, and died June 18, 1749, in his seventy–eighth year.

Of his personal character all that I have heard is, that he was eminent for bravery and skill in the sword, and that in conversation he was solemn and pompous. He had great sensibility of censure, if judgment may be made by a single story which I heard long ago from Mr. Ing, a gentleman of great eminence in Staffordshire. "Philips," said he, "was once at table, when I asked him, 'How came thy king of Epirus to drive oxen, and to say, "I'm goaded on by love"?' After which question he never spoke again."

Of The Distressed Mother not much is pretended to be his own, and therefore it is no subject of criticism: his other two tragedies, I believe, are not below mediocrity, nor above it. Among the poems comprised in the late Collection, the "Letter from Denmark" may be justly praised; the Pastorals, which by the writer of the Guardian were ranked as one of the four genuine productions of the rustic Muse, cannot surely be despicable. That they exhibit a mode of life which did not exist, nor ever existed, is not to be objected: the supposition of such a state is allowed to be pastoral. In his other poems he cannot be denied the praise of lines sometimes elegant; but he has seldom much force or much

54

comprehension. The pieces that please best are those which, from Pope and Pope's adherents, procured him the name of "Namby–Pamby," the poems of short lines, by which he paid his court to all ages and characters, from Walpole the "steerer of the realm," to Miss Pulteney in the nursery. The numbers are smooth and sprightly, and the diction is seldom faulty. They are not loaded with much thought, yet, if they had been written by Addison, they would have had admirers: little things are not valued but when they are done by those who can do greater.

In his translations from "Pindar" he found the art of reaching all the obscurity of the Theban bard, however he may fall below his sublimity; he will be allowed, if he has less fire, to have more smoke. He has added nothing to English poetry, yet at least half his book deserves to be read: perhaps he valued most himself that part which the critic would reject.

WEST.

Gilbert West is one of the writers of whom I regret my inability to give a sufficient account; the intelligence which my inquiries have obtained is general and scanty. He was the son of the Rev. Dr. West; perhaps him who published "Pindar" at Oxford about the beginning of this century. His mother was sister to Sir Richard Temple, afterwards Lord Cobham. His father, purposing to educate him for the Church, sent him first to Eton, and afterwards to Oxford; but he was seduced to a more airy mode of life, by a commission in a troop of horse, procured him by his uncle. He continued some time in the army, though it is reasonable to suppose that he never sunk into a mere soldier, nor ever lost the love, or much neglected the pursuit, of learning; and afterwards, finding himself more inclined to civil employment, he laid down his commission, and engaged in business under the Lord Townshend, then Secretary of State, with whom he attended the King to Hanover.

His adherence to Lord Townshend ended in nothing but a nomination (May, 1729) to be Clerk–Extraordinary of the Privy Council, which produced no immediate profit; for it only placed him in a state of expectation and right of succession, and it was very long before a vacancy admitted him to profit.

Soon afterwards he married, and settled himself in a very pleasant house at Wickham, in Kent, where he devoted himself to learning and to piety. Of his learning the late

Collection exhibits evidence, which would have been yet fuller if the dissertations which accompany his version of "Pindar" had not been improperly omitted. Of his piety the influence has, I hope, been extended far by his "Observations on the Resurrection," published in 1747, for which the University of Oxford created him a Doctor of Laws, by diploma (March 30, 1748), and would doubtless have reached yet further had he lived to complete what he had for some time meditated—the "Evidences of the Truth of the New Testament." Perhaps it may not be without effect to tell that he read the prayers of the public Liturgy every morning to his family, and that on Sunday evening he called his servants into the parlour and read to them first a sermon and then prayers. Crashaw is now not the only maker of verses to whom may be given the two venerable names of Poet and Saint. He was very often visited by Lyttelton and Pitt, who, when they were weary of faction and debates, used at Wickham to find books and quiet, a decent table, and literary conversation. There is at Wickham a walk made by Pitt; and, what is of far more importance, at Wickham, Lyttelton received that conviction which produced his "Dissertation on St. Paul." These two illustrious friends had for a while listened to the blandishments of infidelity; and when West's book was published, it was bought by some who did not know his change of opinion, in expectation of new objections against Christianity; and as infidels do not want malignity, they revenged the disappointment by calling him a Methodist.

Mr. West's income was not large; and his friends endeavoured, but without success, to obtain an augmentation. It is reported that the education of the young Prince was offered to him, but that he required a more extensive power of superintendence than it was thought proper to allow him. In time, however, his revenue was improved; he lived to have one of the lucrative clerkships of the Privy Council (1752); and Mr. Pitt at last had it in his power to make him Treasurer of Chelsea Hospital. He was now sufficiently rich; but wealth came too late to be long enjoyed; nor could it secure him from the calamities of life; he lost (1755) his only son; and the year after (March 26) a stroke of the palsy brought to the grave one of the few poets to whom the grave might be without its terrors.

Of his translations I have only compared the first Olympic Ode with the original, and found my expectation surpassed, both by its elegance and its exactness. He does not confine himself to his author's train of stanzas; for he saw that the difference of languages required a different mode of versification. The first strophe is eminently happy; in the second he has a little strayed from Pindar's meaning, who says, "If thou, my soul, wishest to speak of games, look not in the desert sky for a planet hotter than the sun; nor shall we tell of nobler games than those of Olympia." He is sometimes too paraphrastical. Pindar bestows upon Hiero an epithet which, in one word, signifies DELIGHTING IN HORSES; a word which, in the translation, generates these lines:—

"Hiero's royal brows, whose care
  Tends the courser's noble breed,
Pleased to nurse the pregnant mare,
  Pleased to train the youthful steed."

Pindar says of Pelops, that "he came alone in the dark to the White Sea;" and West—

"Near the billow–beaten side
Of the foam–besilvered main,
Darkling, and alone, he stood:"

which, however, is less exuberant than the former passage.

A work of this kind must, in a minute examination, discover many imperfections; but West's version, so far as I have considered it, appears to be the product of great labour and great abilities.

His "Institution of the Garter" (1742) is written with sufficient knowledge of the manners that prevailed in the age to which it is referred, and with great elegance of diction; but, for want of a process of events, neither knowledge nor elegance preserves the reader from weariness.

His "Imitations of Spenser" are very successfully performed, both with respect to the metre, the language, and the fiction; and being engaged at once by the excellence of the sentiments, and the artifice of the copy, the mind has two amusements together. But such compositions are not to be reckoned among the great achievements of intellect, because their effect is local and temporary; they appeal not to reason or passion, but to memory, and presuppose an accidental or artificial state of mind. An imitation of Spenser is nothing to a reader, however acute, by whom Spenser has never been perused. Works of this kind may deserve praise, as proofs of great industry and great nicety of observation; but the highest praise, the praise of genius, they cannot claim. The noblest beauties of art are those of which the effect is co–extended with rational nature, or at least with the whole circle of polished life; what is less than this can be only pretty, the plaything of fashion, and the amusement of a day.

There is in the Adventurer a paper of verses given to one of the authors as Mr. West's, and supposed to have been written by him. It should not be concealed, however, that it is printed with Mr. Jago's name in Dodsley's Collection, and is mentioned as his in a letter of Shenstone's. Perhaps West gave it without naming the author, and Hawkesworth, receiving it from him, thought it his; for his he thought it, as he told me, and as he tells the public.

COLLINS.

William Collins was born at Chichester, on the 25th day of December, about 1720. His father was a hatter of good reputation. He was in 1733, as Dr. Warton has kindly informed me, admitted scholar of Winchester College, where he was educated by Dr. Burton. His English exercises were better than his Latin. He first courted the notice of the public by some verses to a "Lady weeping," published in The Gentleman's Magazine (January, 1739).

In 1740 he stood first in the list of the scholars to be received in succession at New College, but unhappily there was no vacancy. He became a Commoner of Queen's College, probably with a scanty maintenance; but was, in about half a year, elected a Demy of Magdalen College, where he continued till he had taken a Bachelor's degree, and then suddenly left the University; for what reason I know not that he told.

He now (about 1744) came to London a literary adventurer, with many projects in his head, and very little money in his pocket. He designed many works; but his great fault was irresolution; or the frequent calls of immediate necessity broke his scheme, and suffered him to pursue no settled purpose. A man doubtful of his dinner, or trembling at a creditor, is not much disposed to abstracted meditation or remote inquiries. He published proposals for a "History of the Revival of Learning;" and I have heard him speak with great kindness of Leo X., and with keen resentment of his tasteless successor. But probably not a page of his history was ever written. He planned several tragedies, but he only planned them. He wrote now and then odes and other poems, and did something, however little. About this time I fell into his company. His appearance was decent and manly; his knowledge considerable, his views extensive, his conversation elegant, and his disposition cheerful. By degrees I gained his confidence; and one day was admitted to him when he was immured by a bailiff that was prowling in the street. On this occasion recourse was had to the booksellers, who, on the credit of a translation of Aristotle's "Poetics," which he engaged to write with a large commentary, advanced as much money as enabled him to escape into the country. He showed me the guineas safe in his hand. Soon afterwards his uncle, Mr. Martin, a lieutenant–colonel, left him about 2000 pounds; a sum which Collins could scarcely think exhaustible, and which he did not live to exhaust. The guineas were then repaid, and the translation neglected. But man is not born for happiness. Collins, who, while he studied to live, felt no evil but poverty, no sooner lived to study than his life was assailed by more dreadful calamities—disease and insanity.

Having formerly written his character, while perhaps it was yet more distinctly impressed upon my memory, I shall insert it here.

"Mr. Collins was a man of extensive literature, and of vigorous faculties. He was acquainted not only with the learned tongues, but with the Italian, French, and Spanish languages. He had employed his mind chiefly on works of fiction, and subjects of fancy; and, by indulging some peculiar habits of thought, was eminently delighted with those flights of imagination which pass the bounds of nature, and to which the mind is reconciled only by a passive acquiescence in popular traditions. He loved fairies, genii, giants, and monsters; he delighted to rove through the meanders of enchantment, to gaze on the magnificence of golden palaces, to repose by the waterfalls of Elysian gardens. This was, however, the character rather of his inclination than his genius; the grandeur of wildness, and the novelty of extravagance, were always desired by him, but not always attained. Yet, as diligence is never wholly lost, if his efforts sometimes caused harshness and obscurity, they likewise produced in happier moments sublimity and splendour. This idea which he had formed of excellence led him to Oriental fictions and allegorical imagery, and, perhaps, while he was intent upon description, he did not sufficiently cultivate sentiment. His poems are the productions of a mind not deficient in fire, nor unfurnished with knowledge either of books or life, but somewhat obstructed in its progress by deviation in quest of mistaken beauties.

"His morals were pure, and his opinions pious; in a long continuance of poverty, and long habits of dissipation, it cannot be expected that any character should be exactly uniform.

There is a degree of want by which the freedom of agency is almost destroyed; and long association with fortuitous companions will at last relax the strictness of truth, and abate the fervour of sincerity. That this man, wise and virtuous as he was, passed always unentangled through the snares of life, it would be prejudice and temerity to affirm; but it may be said that at least he preserved the source of action unpolluted, that his principles were never shaken, that his distinctions of right and wrong were never confounded, and that his faults had nothing of malignity or design, but proceeded from some unexpected pressure, or casual temptation.

"The latter part of his life cannot be remembered but with pity and sadness. He languished some years under that depression of mind which enchains the faculties without destroying them, and leaves reason the knowledge of right without the power of pursuing it. These clouds which he perceived gathering on his intellect he endeavoured to disperse by travel, and passed into France; but found himself constrained to yield to his malady, and returned. He was for some time confined in a house of lunatics, and afterwards retired to the care of his sister in Chichester, where death, in 1756, came to his relief.

"After his return from France, the writer of this character paid him a visit at Islington, where he was waiting for his sister, whom he had directed to meet him. There was then nothing of disorder discernible in his mind by any but himself; but he had withdrawn from study, and travelled with no other book than an English Testament, such as children carry to the school. When his friend took it into his hand, out of curiosity to see what companion a man of letters had chosen, 'I have but one book,' said Collins, 'but that is the best.'"

Such was the fate of Collins, with whom I once delighted to converse, and whom I yet remember with tenderness.

He was visited at Chichester, in his last illness, by his learned friends Dr. Warton and his brother, to whom he spoke with disapprobation of his "Oriental Eclogues," as not sufficiently expressive of Asiatic manners, and called them his "Irish Eclogues." He showed them, at the same time, an ode inscribed to Mr. John Home, on the superstitions of the Highlands, which they thought superior to his other works, but which no search has yet found. His disorder was no alienation of mind, but general laxity and feebleness—a deficiency rather of his vital than his intellectual powers. What he spoke wanted neither judgment nor spirit; but a few minutes exhausted him, so that he was forced to rest upon the couch, till a short cessation restored his powers, and he was again able to talk with his former vigour. The approaches of this dreadful malady he began to feel soon after his uncle's death; and, with the usual weakness of men so diseased, eagerly snatched that temporary relief with which the table and the bottle flatter and seduce. But his health continually declined, and he grew more and more burthensome to himself.

To what I have formerly said of his writings may be added, that his diction was often harsh, unskilfully laboured, and injudiciously selected. He affected the obsolete when it was not worthy of revival: and he puts his words out of the common order, seeming to think, with some later candidates for fame, that not to write prose is certainly to write poetry. His lines commonly are of slow motion, clogged and impeded with clusters of consonants. As men are often esteemed who cannot be loved, so the poetry of Collins may sometimes extort praise when it gives little pleasure.

Mr. Collins's first production is added here from the Poetical Calendar:—

TO MISS AURELIA C—R,

ON HER WEEPING AT HER SISTER'S WEDDING.

"Cease, fair Aurelia, cease to mourn;
  Lament not Hannah's happy state;
You may be happy in your turn,
  And seize the treasure you regret.
With Love united Hymen stands,
  And softly whispers to your charms,
'Meet but your lover in my bands,
  You'll find your sister in his arms.'"

DYER.

John Dyer, of whom I have no other account to give than his own letters, published with Hughes's correspondence, and the notes added by the editor, have afforded me, was born in 1700, the second son of Robert Dyer of Aberglasney, in Caermarthenshire, a solicitor of great capacity and note. He passed through Westminster school under the care of Dr. Freind, and was then called home to be instructed in his father's profession. But his father died soon, and he took no delight in the study of the law; but, having always amused himself with drawing, resolved to turn painter, and became pupil to Mr. Richardson, an artist then of high reputation, but now better known by his books than by his pictures.

Having studied a while under his master, he became, as he tells his friend, an itinerant painter, and wandered about South Wales and the parts adjacent; but he mingled poetry with painting, and about 1727 [1726] printed "Grongar Hill" in Lewis's Miscellany. Being, probably, unsatisfied with his own proficiency, he, like other painters, travelled to Italy; and coming back in 1740, published the "Ruins of Rome." If his poem was written soon after his return, he did not make use of his acquisitions in painting, whatever they might be; for decline of health and love of study determined him to the Church. He therefore entered into orders; and, it seems, married about the same time a lady of the name of Ensor; "whose grandmother," says he, "was a Shakspeare, descended from a brother of everybody's Shakspeare;" by her, in 1756, he had a son and three daughters living.

His ecclesiastical provision was for a long time but slender. His first patron, Mr. Harper, gave him, in 1741, Calthorp in Leicestershire, of eighty pounds a year, on which he lived ten years, and then exchanged it for Belchford, in Lincolnshire, of seventy–five. His condition now began to mend. In 1751 Sir John Heathcote gave him Coningsby, of one hundred and forty pounds a year; and in 1755 the Chancellor added Kirkby, of one hundred and ten. He complains that the repair of the house at Coningsby, and other expenses, took away the profit. In 1757 he published "The Fleece," his greatest poetical work; of which I will not suppress a ludicrous story. Dodsley the bookseller was one day mentioning it to a critical visitor, with more expectation of success than the other could easily admit. In the conversation the author's age was asked; and being represented as advanced in life, "He will," said the critic, "be buried in woollen." He did not indeed long survive that publication, nor long enjoy the increase of his preferments, for in 1758 he died.

Dyer is not a poet of bulk or dignity sufficient to require an elaborate criticism. "Grongar Hill" is the happiest of his productions: it is not indeed very accurately written; but the scenes which it displays are so pleasing, the images which they raise are so welcome to the mind, and the reflections of the writer so consonant to the general sense or experience of mankind, that when it is once read, it will be read again. The idea of the "Ruins of Rome" strikes more, but pleases less, and the title raises greater expectation than the performance gratifies. Some passages, however, are conceived with the mind of a poet; as when, in the neighbourhood of dilapidating edifices, he says,

"The Pilgrim oft
At dead of night, 'mid his orison hears
Aghast the voice of Time, disparting tow'rs
Tumbling all precipitate down dashed,
Rattling around, loud thund'ring to the Moon."

Of "The Fleece," which never became popular, and is now universally neglected, I can say little that is likely to recall it to attention. The woolcomber and the poet appear to me such discordant natures, that an attempt to bring them together is to COUPLE THE SERPENT WITH THE FOWL. When Dyer, whose mind was not unpoetical, has done his utmost, by interesting his reader in our native commodity by interspersing rural imagery, and incidental digressions, by clothing small images in great words, and by all the writer's arts of delusion, the meanness naturally adhering, and the irreverence habitually annexed to trade and manufacture, sink him under insuperable oppression; and the disgust which blank verse, encumbering and encumbered, superadds to an unpleasing subject, soon repels the reader, however willing to be pleased.

Let me, however, honestly report whatever may counterbalance this weight of censure. I have been told that Akenside, who, upon a poetical question, has a right to be heard, said, "That he would regulate his opinion of the reigning taste by the fate of Dyer's 'Fleece;' for, if that were ill-received, he should not think it any longer reasonable to expect fame from excellence."

SHENSTONE.

William Shenstone, the son of Thomas Shenstone and Anne Pen, was born in November, 1714, at the Leasowes in Hales-Owen, one of those insulated districts which, in the division of the kingdom, was appended, for some reason not now discoverable, to a distant county; and which, though surrounded by Warwickshire and Worcestershire, belongs to Shropshire, though perhaps thirty miles distant from any other part of it. He

Lives of the Poets

learned to read of an old dame, whom his poem of the "Schoolmistress" has delivered to posterity; and soon received such delight from books, that he was always calling for fresh entertainment, and expected that, when any of the family went to market, a new book should be brought him, which, when it came, was in fondness carried to bed and laid by him. It is said, that, when his request had been neglected, his mother wrapped up a piece of wood of the same form, and pacified him for the night. As he grew older, he went for a while to the Grammar–school in Hales–Owen, and was placed afterwards with Mr. Crumpton, an eminent schoolmaster at Solihul, where he distinguished himself by the quickness of his progress.

When he was young (June, 1724) he was deprived of his father, and soon after (August, 1726) of his grandfather; and was, with his brother, who died afterwards unmarried, left to the care of his grandmother, who managed the estate.

From school he was sent in 1732 to Pembroke College in Oxford, a society which for half a century has been eminent for English poetry and elegant literature. Here it appears that he found delight and advantage; for he continued his name in the book ten years, though he took no degree. After the first four years he put on the civilian's gown, but without showing any intention to engage in the profession. About the time when he went to Oxford, the death of his grandmother devolved his affairs to the care of the Rev. Mr. Dolman, of Brome in Staffordshire, whose attention he always mentioned with gratitude. At Oxford he employed himself upon English poetry; and in 1737 published a small Miscellany, without his name. He then for a time wandered about, to acquaint himself with life, and was sometimes at London, sometimes at Bath, or any other place of public resort; but he did not forget his poetry. He published in 1741 his "Judgment of Hercules," addressed to Mr. Lyttelton, whose interest he supported with great warmth at an election: this was next year followed by the "Schoolmistress."

Mr. Dolman, to whose care he was indebted for his ease and leisure, died in 1745, and the care of his own fortune now fell upon him. He tried to escape it awhile, and lived at his house with his tenants, who were distantly related; but, finding that imperfect possession inconvenient, he took the whole estate into his own hands, more to the improvement of its beauty than the increase of its produce. Now was excited his delight in rural pleasures and his ambition of rural elegance; he began from this time to point his prospects, to diversify his surface, to entangle his walks, and to wind his waters, which he did with such judgment and such fancy as made his little domain the envy of the great and the

64

admiration of the skilful; a place to be visited by travellers and copied by designers. Whether to plant a walk in undulating curves, and to place a bench at every turn where there is an object to catch the view, to make the water run where it will be heard, and to stagnate where it will be seen, to leave intervals where the eye will be pleased, and to thicken the plantation where there is something to be hidden, demands any great powers of mind, I will not inquire: perhaps a sullen and surly spectator may think such performances rather the sport than the business of human reason. But it must be at least confessed that to embellish the form of Nature is an innocent amusement, and some praise must be allowed, by the most supercilious observer, to him who does best what such multitudes are contending to do well.

This praise was the praise of Shenstone; but, like all other modes of felicity, it was not enjoyed without its abatements. Lyttelton was his neighbour and his rival, whose empire, spacious and opulent, looked with disdain on the PETTY STATE that APPEARED BEHIND IT. For a while the inhabitants of Hagley affected to tell their acquaintance of the little fellow that was trying to make himself admired; but when by degrees the Leasowes forced themselves into notice, they took care to defeat the curiosity which they could not suppress by conducting their visitants perversely to inconvenient points of view, and introducing them at the wrong end of a walk to detect a deception; injuries of which Shenstone would heavily complain. Where there is emulation there will be vanity; and where there is vanity there will be folly.

The pleasure of Shenstone was all in his eye; he valued what he valued merely for its looks. Nothing raised his indignation more than to ask if there were any fishes in his water. His house was mean, and he did not improve it; his care was of his grounds. When he came home from his walks, he might find his floors flooded by a shower through the broken roof; but could spare no money for its reparation. In time his expenses brought clamours about him that overpowered the lamb's bleat and the linnet's song, and his groves were haunted by beings very different from fauns and fairies. He spent his estate in adorning it, and his death was probably hastened by his anxieties. He was a lamp that spent its oil in blazing. It is said that, if he had lived a little longer, he would have been assisted by a pension: such bounty could not have been ever more properly bestowed; but that it was ever asked is not certain; it is too certain that it never was enjoyed. He died at Leasowes, of a putrid fever, about five on Friday morning, February 11, 1763, and was buried by the side of his brother in the churchyard of Hales– Owen.

He was never married, though he might have obtained the lady, whoever she was, to whom his "Pastoral Ballad" was addressed. He is represented by his friend Dodsley as a man of great tenderness and generosity, kind to all that were within his influence; but, if once offended, not easily appeased; inattentive to economy, and careless of his expenses; in his person he was larger than the middle–size, with something clumsy in his form; very negligent of his clothes, and remarkable for wearing his grey hair in a particular manner, for he held that the fashion was no rule of dress, and that every man was to suit his appearance to his natural form. His mind was not very comprehensive, nor his curiosity active; he had no value for those parts of knowledge which he had not himself cultivated. His life was unstained by any crime. The "Elegy on Jesse," which has been supposed to relate an unfortunate and criminal amour of his own, was known by his friends to have been suggested by the story of Miss Godfrey in Richardson's "Pamela."

What Gray thought of his character, from the perusal of his Letters, was this:—

"I have read, too, an octavo volume of Shenstone's Letters. Poor man! he was always wishing for money, for fame, and other distinctions; and his whole philosophy consisted in living against his will in retirement, and in a place which his taste had adorned, but which he only enjoyed when people of note came to see and commend it. His correspondence is about nothing else but this place and his own writings, with two or three neighbouring clergymen, who wrote verses too."

His poems consist of elegies, odes, and ballads, humorous sallies, and moral pieces. His conception of an Elegy he has in his Preface very judiciously and discriminately explained. It is, according to his account, the effusion of a contemplative mind, sometimes plaintive, and always serious, and therefore superior to the glitter of slight ornaments. His compositions suit not ill to this description. His topics of praise are the domestic virtues, and his thoughts are pure and simple, but wanting combination; they want variety. The peace of solitude, the innocence of inactivity, and the unenvied security of an humble station, can fill but a few pages. That of which the essence is uniformity will be soon described. His elegies have, therefore, too much resemblance of each other. The lines are sometimes, such as Elegy requires, smooth and easy; but to this praise his claim is not constant; his diction is often harsh, improper, and affected, his words ill–coined or ill– chosen, and his phrase unskilfully inverted.

Lives of the Poets

The Lyric Poems are almost all of the light and airy kind, such as trip lightly and nimbly along, without the load of any weighty meaning. From these, however, "Rural Elegance" has some right to be excepted. I once heard it praised by a very learned lady; and, though the lines are irregular, and the thoughts diffused with too much verbosity, yet it cannot be denied to contain both philosophical argument and poetical spirit. Of the rest I cannot think any excellent; the "Skylark" pleases me best, which has, however, more of the epigram than of the ode.

But the four parts of his "Pastoral Ballad" demand particular notice. I cannot but regret that it is pastoral: an intelligent reader acquainted with the scenes of real life sickens at the mention of the CROOK, the PIPE, the SHEEP, and the KIDS, which it is not necessary to bring forward to notice; for the poet's art is selection, and he ought to show the beauties without the grossness of the country life. His stanza seems to have been chosen in imitation of Rowe's "Despairing Shepherd." In the first are two passages, to which if any mind denies its sympathy, it has no acquaintance with love or nature:—

"I prized every hour that went by,
  Beyond all that had pleased me before:
But now they are past, and I sigh,
  And I grieve that I prized them no more.

When forced the fair nymph to forego,
  What anguish I felt in my heart!
Yet I thought (but it might not be so)
  'Twas with pain that she saw me depart.

She gazed, as I slowly withdrew,
  My path I could hardly discern;
So sweetly she bade me adieu,
  I thought that she bade me return."

In the second this passage has its prettiness; though it be not equal to the former:—

"I have found out a gift for my fair:
  I have found where the wood pigeons breed:
But let me that plunder forbear,

She will say 'twas a barbarous deed:

For he ne'er could be true, she averred,
  Who could rob a poor bird of its young;
And I loved her the more when I heard
  Such tenderness fall from her tongue."

In the third he mentions the common–places of amorous poetry with some address:—

"'Tis his with mock passion to glow!
  'Tis his in smooth tales to unfold,
How her face is as bright as the snow,
  And her bosom, be sure, is as cold:

How the nightingales labour the strain,
  With the notes of this charmer to vie:
How they vary their accents in vain,
  Repine at her triumphs, and die."

In the fourth I find nothing better than this natural strain of Hope:—

"Alas! from the day that we met,
  What hope of an end to my woes,
When I cannot endure to forget
  The glance that undid my repose?

Yet Time may diminish the pain:
  The flower, and the shrub, and the tree,
Which I reared for her pleasure in vain,
  In time may have comfort for me."

His "Levities" are by their title exempted from the severities of criticism, yet it may be remarked in a few words that his humour is sometimes gross, and seldom sprightly.

Of the Moral Poems, the first is the "Choice of Hercules," from Xenophon. The numbers are smooth, the diction elegant, and the thoughts just; but something of vigour is still to

68

be wished, which it might have had by brevity and compression. His "Fate of Delicacy" has an air of gaiety, but not a very pointed and general moral. His blank verses, those that can read them, may probably find to be like the blank verses of his neighbours. "Love and Honour" is derived from the old ballad, "Did you not hear of a Spanish Lady?"—I wish it well enough to wish it were in rhyme.

The "Schoolmistress," of which I know not what claim it has to stand among the Moral Works, is surely the most pleasing of Shenstone's performances. The adoption of a particular style, in light and short compositions, contributes much to the increase of pleasure: we are entertained at once with two imitations of nature in the sentiments, of the original author in the style, and between them the mind is kept in perpetual employment.

The general recommendation of Shenstone is easiness and simplicity; his general defect is want of comprehension and variety. Had his mind been better stored with knowledge, whether he could have been great, I know not; he could certainly have been agreeable.

YOUNG.

The following life was written, at my request, by a gentleman (Mr. Herbert Croft) who had better information than I could easily have obtained; and the public will perhaps wish that I had solicited and obtained more such favours from him:—

"Dear Sir,—In consequence of our different conversations about authentic materials for the Life of Young, I send you the following details:"—

Of great men something must always be said to gratify curiosity. Of the illustrious author of the "Night Thoughts" much has been told of which there never could have been proofs, and little care appears to have been taken to tell that of which proofs, with little trouble, might have been procured.

Edward Young was born at Upham, near Winchester, in June, 1681. He was the son of Edward Young, at that time Fellow of Winchester College, and Rector of Upham, who was the son of Jo. Young, of Woodhay, in Berkshire, styled by Wood, GENTLEMAN. In September, 1682, the poet's father was collated to the prebend of Gillingham Minor, in the church of Sarum, by Bishop Ward. When Ward's faculties were impaired through age, his duties were necessarily performed by others. We learn from Wood that, at a visitation of Sprat's, July the 12th, 1686, the prebendary preached a Latin sermon, afterwards published, with which the Bishop was so pleased, that he told the chapter he was concerned to find the preacher had one of the worst prebends in their Church. Some time after this, in consequence of his merit and reputation, or of the interest of Lord Bradford, to whom, in 1702, he dedicated two volumes of sermons, he was appointed chaplain to King William and Queen Mary, and preferred to the Deanery of Sarum. Jacob, who wrote in 1720, says, "he was Chaplain and Clerk of the Closet to the late Queen, who honoured him by standing godmother to the poet." His Fellowship of Winchester he resigned in favour of a gentleman of the name of Harris, who married his only daughter. The Dean died at Sarum, after a short illness, in 1705, in the sixty-third year of his age. On the Sunday after his decease, Bishop Burnet preached at the cathedral, and began his sermon with saying, "Death has been of late walking round us, and making breach upon breach upon us, and has now carried away the head of this body with a stroke, so that he, whom you saw a week ago distributing the holy mysteries, is now laid in the dust. But he still lives in the many excellent directions he has left us both how to live and how to die."

The dean placed his son upon the foundation at Winchester College, where he had himself been educated. At this school Edward Young remained till the election after his eighteenth birthday, the period at which those upon the foundation are superannuated. Whether he did not betray his abilities early in life, or his masters had not skill enough to discover in their pupil any marks of genius for which he merited reward, or no vacancy at Oxford offered them an opportunity to bestow upon him the reward provided for merit by William of Wykeham; certain it is, that to an Oxford fellowship our poet did not succeed. By chance, or by choice, New College cannot claim the honour of numbering among its fellows him who wrote the "Night Thoughts."

On the 13th of October, 1703, he was entered an independent member of New College, that he might live at little expense in the warden's lodgings, who was a particular friend of his father's, till he should be qualified to stand for a fellowship at All Souls. In a few months the warden of New College died. He then removed to Corpus College. The president of this society, from regard also for his father, invited him thither, in order to lessen his academical expenses. In 1708 he was nominated to a law-fellowship at All Souls by Archbishop Tenison, into whose hands it came by devolution. Such repeated patronage, while it justifies Burnet's praise of the father, reflects credit on the conduct of the son. The manner in which it was exerted seems to prove that the father did not leave behind him much wealth.

On the 23rd of April, 1714, Young took his degree of bachelor of civil laws, and his doctor's degree on the 10th of June, 1719. Soon after he went to Oxford he discovered, it is said, an inclination for pupils. Whether he ever commenced tutor is not known. None has hitherto boasted to have received his academical instruction from the author of "Night Thoughts." It is probable that his College was proud of him no less as a scholar than as a poet; for in 1716, when the foundation of the Codrington Library was laid, two years after he had taken his bachelor's degree, Young was appointed to speak the Latin oration. This is at least particular for being dedicated in English "To the Ladies of the Codrington Family." To these ladies he says "that he was unavoidably flung into a singularity, by being obliged to write an epistle dedicatory void of commonplace, and such an one was never published before by any author whatever; that this practice absolved them from any obligation of reading what was presented to them; and that the bookseller approved of it, because it would make people stare, was absurd enough and perfectly right." Of this oration there is no appearance in his own edition of his works; and prefixed to an edition by Curll and Tonson, in 1741, is a letter from Young to Curll, if we may credit Curll, dated December the 9th, 1739, wherein he says that he has not leisure to review what he formerly wrote, and adds, "I have not the 'Epistle to Lord Lansdowne.' If you will take my advice, I would have you omit that, and the oration on Codrington. I think the collection will sell better without them."

There are who relate that, when first Young found himself independent, and his own master at All Souls, he was not the ornament to religion and morality which he afterwards became. The authority of his father, indeed, had ceased, some time before, by his death; and Young was certainly not ashamed to be patronised by the infamous Wharton. But Wharton befriended in Young, perhaps, the poet, and particularly the tragedian. If virtuous authors must be patronised only by virtuous peers, who shall point them out? Yet Pope is said by Ruffhead to have told Warburton that "Young had much of a sublime genius, though without common sense; so that his genius, having no guide, was perpetually liable to degenerate into bombast. This made him pass a FOOLISH YOUTH, the sport of peers and poets: but his having a very good heart enabled him to support the clerical character when he assumed it, first with decency, and afterwards with honour."

They who think ill of Young's morality in the early part of his life may perhaps be wrong; but Tindal could not err in his opinion of Young's warmth and ability in the cause of religion. Tindal used to spend much of his time at All Souls. "The other boys," said the atheist, "I can always answer, because I always know whence they have their arguments, which I have read a hundred times; but that fellow Young is continually pestering me with something of his own."

After all, Tindal and the censurers of Young may be reconcilable. Young might, for two or three years, have tried that kind of life, in which his natural principles would not suffer him to wallow long. If this were so, he has left behind him not only his evidence in favour of virtue, but the potent testimony of experience against vice. We shall soon see that one of his earliest productions was more serious than what comes from the generality of unfledged poets.

Young perhaps ascribed the good fortune of Addison to the "Poem to his Majesty," presented with a copy of verses, to Somers: and hoped that he also might soar to wealth and honours on wings of the same kind. His first poetical flight was when Queen Anne called up to the House of Lords the sons of the Earls of Northampton and Aylesbury, and added, in one day, ten others to the number of Peers. In order to reconcile the people to one, at least, of the new lords, he published, in 1712, "An Epistle to the Right Honourable George Lord Lansdowne." In this composition the poet pours out his panegyric with the extravagance of a young man, who thinks his present stock of wealth will never be exhausted. The poem seems intended also to reconcile the public to the late peace. This is endeavoured to be done by showing that men are slain in war, and that in peace "harvests wave, and commerce swells her sail." If this be humanity, for which he meant it, is it politics? Another purpose of this epistle appears to have been to prepare the public for the reception of some tragedy he might have in hand. His lordship's patronage, he says, will not let him "repent his passion for the stage;" and the particular praise bestowed on Othello and Oroonoko looks as if some such character as Zanga was even then in contemplation. The affectionate mention of the death of his friend Harrison of New College, at the close of this poem, is an instance of Young's art, which displayed itself so wonderfully some time afterwards in the "Night Thoughts," of making the public a party in his private sorrow. Should justice call upon you to censure this poem, it ought at least to be remembered that he did not insert it in his works; and that in the letter to Curll, as we have seen, he advises its omission. The booksellers, in the late body of English poetry, should have distinguished what was deliberately rejected by the respective authors. This I shall be careful to do with regard to Young. "I think," says he, "the following pieces in FOUR volumes to be the most excusable of all that I have written; and I wish LESS APOLOGY was less needful for these. As there is no recalling what is got abroad, the pieces here republished I have revised and corrected, and rendered them as PARDONABLE as it was in my power to do."

Shall the gates of repentance be shut only against literary sinners?

When Addison published "Cato" in 1713, Young had the honour of prefixing to it a recommendatory copy of verses. This is one of the pieces which the author of the "Night Thoughts" did not republish.

On the appearance of his poem on the "Last Day," Addison did not return Young's compliment; but "The Englishman" of October 29, 1713, which was probably written by Addison, speaks handsomely of this poem. The "Last Day" was published soon after the peace. The Vice–Chancellor's imprimatur (for it was printed at Oxford) is dated the 19th, 1713. From the exordium, Young appears to have spent some time on the composition of it. While other bards "with Britain's hero set their souls on fire," he draws, he says, a deeper scene. Marlborough HAD BEEN considered by Britain as her HERO; but, when the "Last Day" was published, female cabal had blasted for a time the laurels of Blenheim. This serious poem was finished by Young as early as 1710, before he was thirty; for part of it is printed in the Tatler. It was inscribed to the queen, in a dedication, which, for some reason, he did not admit into his works. It tells her that his only title to the great honour he now does himself is the obligation which he formerly received from her royal indulgence. Of this obligation nothing is now known, unless he alluded to her being his godmother. He is said indeed to have been engaged at a settled stipend as a writer for the Court. In Swift's "Rhapsody on Poetry" are these lines, speaking of the Court:—

"Whence Gay was banished in disgrace,
Where Pope will never show his face,
Where Y—— must torture his invention
To flatter knaves, or lose his pension."

That Y—— means Young seems clear from four other lines in the same poem:—

"Attend, ye Popes, and Youngs, and Gays,
  And tune your harps and strew your bays;
  Your panegyrics here provide;
  You cannot err on flattery's side."

Yet who shall say with certainty that Young was a pensioner? In all modern periods of this country, have not the writers on one side been regularly called Hirelings, and on the other Patriots?

Of the dedication the complexion is clearly political. It speaks in the highest terms of the late peace; it gives her Majesty praise indeed for her victories, but says that the author is more pleased to see her rise from this lower world, soaring above the clouds, passing the first and second heavens, and leaving the fixed stars behind her; nor will he lose her there, he says, but keep her still in view through the boundless spaces on the other side of creation, in her journey towards eternal bliss, till he behold the heaven of heavens open, and angels receiving and conveying her still onward from the stretch of his imagination, which tires in her pursuit, and falls back again to earth.

The queen was soon called away from this lower world, to a place where human praise or human flattery, even less general than this, are of little consequence. If Young thought the dedication contained only the praise of truth, he should not have omitted it in his works. Was he conscious of the exaggeration of party? Then he should not have written it. The poem itself is not without a glance towards politics, notwithstanding the subject. The cry that the Church was in danger had not yet subsided. The "Last Day," written by a layman, was much approved by the ministry and their friends.

Before the queen's death, "The Force of Religion, or Vanquished Love," was sent into the world. This poem is founded on the execution of Lady Jane Grey and her husband, Lord Guildford, 1554, a story chosen for the subject of a tragedy by Edmund Smith, and wrought into a tragedy by Rowe. The dedication of it to the Countess of Salisbury does not appear in his own edition. He hopes it may be some excuse for his presumption that the story could not have been read without thoughts of the Countess of Salisbury, though it had been dedicated to another. "To behold," he proceeds, "a person ONLY virtuous, stirs in us a prudent regret; to behold a person ONLY amiable to the sight, warms us with a religious indignation; but to turn our eyes to a Countess of Salisbury, gives us pleasure and improvement; it works a sort of miracle, occasions the bias of our nature to fall off

74

from sin, and makes our very senses and affections converts to our religion, and promoters of our duty." His flattery was as ready for the other sex as for ours, and was at least as well adapted.

August the 27th, 1714, Pope writes to his friend Jervas, that he is just arrived from Oxford; that every one is much concerned for the queen's death, but that no panegyrics are ready yet for the king. Nothing like friendship has yet taken place between Pope and Young, for, soon after the event which Pope mentions, Young published a poem on the queen's death, and his Majesty's accession to the throne. It is inscribed to Addison, then secretary to the Lords Justices. Whatever were the obligations which he had formerly received from Anne, the poet appears to aim at something of the same sort from George. Of the poem the intention seems to have been, to show that he had the same extravagant strain of praise for a king as for a queen. To discover, at the very onset of a foreigner's reign, that the gods bless his new subjects in such a king is something more than praise. Neither was this deemed one of his excusable pieces. We do not find it in his works.

Young's father had been well acquainted with Lady Anne Wharton, the first wife of Thomas Wharton, Esq., afterwards Marquis of Wharton; a lady celebrated for her poetical talents by Burnet and by Waller.

To the Dean of Sarum's visitation sermon, already mentioned, were added some verses "by that excellent poetess, Mrs. Anne Wharton," upon its being translated into English, at the instance of Waller by Atwood. Wharton, after he became ennobled, did not drop the son of his old friend. In him, during the short time he lived, Young found a patron, and in his dissolute descendant a friend and a companion. The marquis died in April, 1715. In the beginning of the next year, the young marquis set out upon his travels, from which he returned in about a twelvemonth. The beginning of 1717 carried him to Ireland: where, says the Biographia, "on the score of his extraordinary qualities, he had the honour done him of being admitted, though under age, to take his seat in the House of Lords." With this unhappy character it is not unlikely that Young went to Ireland. From his letter to Richardson on "Original Composition," it is clear he was, at some period of his life, in that country. "I remember," says he, in that letter, speaking of Swift, "as I and others were taking with him an evening walk, about a mile out of Dublin, he stopped short; we passed on; but perceiving he did not follow us, I went back, and found him fixed as a statue, and earnestly gazing upward at a noble elm, which in its uppermost branches was much withered and decayed. Pointing at it, he said, 'I shall be like that tree, I shall die at top.'"

Is it not probable, that this visit to Ireland was paid when he had an opportunity of going thither with his avowed friend and patron?

From "The Englishman" it appears that a tragedy by Young was in the theatre so early as 1713. Yet Busiris was not brought upon Drury Lane stage till 1719. It was inscribed to the Duke of Newcastle, "because the late instances he had received of his grace's undeserved and uncommon favour, in an affair of some consequence, foreign to the theatre, had taken from him the privilege of choosing a patron." The Dedication he afterwards suppressed.

Busiris was followed in the year 1721 by The Revenge. He dedicated this famous tragedy to the Duke of Wharton. "Your Grace," says the Dedication, "has been pleased to make yourself accessory to the following scenes, not only by suggesting the most beautiful incident in them, but by making all possible provision for the success of the whole." That his grace should have suggested the incident to which he alludes, whatever that incident might have been, is not unlikely. The last mental exertion of the superannuated young man, in his quarters at Lerida, in Spain, was some scenes of a tragedy on the story of Mary Queen of Scots.

Dryden dedicated "Marriage a la Mode" to Wharton's infamous relation Rochester, whom he acknowledges not only as the defender of his poetry, but as the promoter of his fortune. Young concludes his address to Wharton thus—"My present fortune is his bounty, and my future his care; which I will venture to say will be always remembered to his honour, since he, I know, intended his generosity as an encouragement to merit, though through his very pardonable partiality to one who bears him so sincere a duty and respect, I happen to receive the benefit of it." That he ever had such a patron as Wharton, Young took all the pains in his power to conceal from the world, by excluding this dedication from his works. He should have remembered that he at the same time concealed his obligation to Wharton for THE MOST BEAUTIFUL INCIDENT in what is surely not his least beautiful composition. The passage just quoted is, in a poem afterwards addressed to Walpole, literally copied:

"Be this thy partial smile from censure free!
'Twas meant for merit, though it fell on me."

Lives of the Poets

While Young, who, in his "Love of Fame," complains grievously how often "dedications wash an AEthiop white," was painting an amiable Duke of Wharton in perishable prose, Pope was, perhaps, beginning to describe the "scorn and wonder of his days" in lasting verse. To the patronage of such a character, had Young studied men as much as Pope, he would have known how little to have trusted. Young, however, was certainly indebted to it for something material; and the duke's regard for Young, added to his lust of praise, procured to All Souls College a donation, which was not forgotten by the poet when he dedicated The Revenge.

It will surprise you to see me cite second Atkins, Case 136, Stiles versus the Attorney–General, March 14, 1740, as authority for the life of a poet. But biographers do not always find such certain guides as the oaths of the persons whom they record. Chancellor Hardwicke was to determine whether two annuities, granted by the Duke of Wharton to Young, were for legal considerations. One was dated the 24th March, 1719, and accounted for his grace's bounty in a style princely and commendable, if not legal—"considering that the public good is advanced by the encouragement of learning and the polite arts, and being pleased therein with the attempts of Dr. Young, in consideration thereof, and of the love I bear him, etc." The other was dated the 10th of July, 1722.

Young, on his examination, swore that he quitted the Exeter family, and refused an annuity of 100 pounds which had been offered him for life if he would continue tutor to Lord Burleigh, upon the pressing solicitations of the Duke of Wharton, and his grace's assurances of providing for him in a much more ample manner. It also appeared that the duke had given him a bond for 600 pounds dated the 15th of March, 1721, in consideration of his taking several journeys, and being at great expenses, in order to be chosen member of the House of Commons, at the duke's desire, and in consideration of his not taking two livings of 200 pounds and 400 pounds in the gift of All Souls College, on his grace's promises of serving and advancing him in the world.

Of his adventures in the Exeter family I am unable to give any account. The attempt to get into Parliament was at Cirencester, where Young stood a contested election. His grace discovered in him talents for oratory as well as for poetry. Nor was this judgment wrong. Young, after he took orders, became a very popular preacher, and was much followed for the grace and animation of his delivery. By his oratorical talents he was once in his life, according to the Biographia, deserted. As he was preaching in his turn at St. James's, he plainly perceived it was out of his power to command the attention of his audience. This so affected the feelings of the preacher, that he sat back in the pulpit, and burst into tears. But we must pursue his poetical life.

In 1719 he lamented the death of Addison, in a letter addressed to their common friend Tickell. For the secret history of the following lines, if they contain any, it is now vain to seek:

"IN JOY ONCE JOINED, in sorrow, now, for years—
Partner in grief, and brother of my tears,
Tickell, accept this verse, thy mournful due."

From your account of Tickell it appears that he and Young used to "communicate to each other whatever verses they wrote, even to the least things."

In 1719 appeared a "Paraphrase on Part of the Book of Job." Parker, to whom it is dedicated, had not long, by means of the seals, been qualified for a patron. Of this work the author's opinion may be known from his letter to Curll: "You seem, in the Collection you propose, to have omitted what I think may claim the first place in it; I mean 'a Translation from part of Job,' printed by Mr. Tonson." The Dedication, which was only suffered to appear in Mr. Tonson's edition, while it speaks with satisfaction of his present retirement, seems to make an unusual struggle to escape from retirement. But every one who sings in the dark does not sing from joy. It is addressed, in no common strain of flattery, to a chancellor, of whom he clearly appears to have had no kind of knowledge.

Of his Satires it would not have been possible to fix the dates without the assistance of first editions, which, as you had occasion to observe in your account of Dryden, are with difficulty found. We must then have referred to the poems, to discover when they were written. For these internal notes of time we should not have referred in vain. The first Satire laments, that "Guilt's chief foe in Addison is fled." The second, addressing himself, asks:—

"Is thy ambition sweating for a rhyme,
Thou unambitious fool, at this late time?
A fool at FORTY is a fool indeed."

Lives of the Poets

The Satires were originally published separately in folio, under the title of "The Universal Passion." These passages fix the appearance of the first to about 1725, the time at which it came out. As Young seldom suffered his pen to dry after he had once dipped it in poetry, we may conclude that he began his Satires soon after he had written the "Paraphrase on Job." The last Satire was certainly finished in the beginning of the year 1726. In December, 1725, the King, in his passage from Helvoetsluys, escaped with great difficulty from a storm by landing at Rye; and the conclusion of the Satire turns the escape into a miracle, in such an encomiastic strain of compliment as poetry too often seeks to pay to royalty. From the sixth of these poems we learn,

"'Midst empire's charms, how Carolina's heart
Glowed with the love of virtue and of art."

Since the grateful poet tells us, in the next couplet,

"Her favour is diffused to that degree,
Excess of goodness! it has dawned on me."

Her Majesty had stood godmother, and given her name, to the daughter of the lady whom Young married in 1731; and had perhaps shown some attention to Lady Elizabeth's future husband.

The fifth Satire, "On Women," was not published till 1727; and the sixth not till 1728.

To these poems, when, in 1728, he gathered them into one publication, he prefixed a Preface, in which he observes that "no man can converse much in the world, but at what he meets with he must either be insensible or grieve, or be angry or smile. Now to smile at it, and turn it into ridicule," he adds, "I think most eligible, as it hurts ourselves least, and gives vice and folly the greatest offence. Laughing at the misconduct of the world will, in a great measure, ease us of any more disagreeable passion about it. One passion is more effectually driven out by another than by reason, whatever some teach." So wrote, and so of course thought, the lively and witty satirist at the grave age of almost fifty, who, many years earlier in life, wrote the "Last Day." After all, Swift pronounced of these Satires, that they should either have been more angry or more merry.

Is it not somewhat singular that Young preserved, without any palliation, this Preface, so bluntly decisive in favour of laughing at the world, in the same collection of his works which contains the mournful, angry, gloomy "Night Thoughts!" At the conclusion of the Preface he applies Plato's beautiful fable of the "Birth of Love" to modern poetry, with the addition, "that Poetry, like Love, is a little subject to blindness, which makes her mistake her way to preferments and honours; and that she retains a dutiful admiration of her father's family; but divides her favours, and generally lives with her mother's relations." Poetry, it is true, did not lead Young to preferments or to honours; but was there not something like blindness in the flattery which he sometimes forced her, and her sister Prose, to utter? She was always, indeed, taught by him to entertain a most dutiful admiration of riches; but surely Young, though nearly related to Poetry, had no connection with her whom Plato makes the mother of Love. That he could not well complain of being related to Poverty appears clearly from the frequent bounties which his gratitude records, and from the wealth which he left behind him. By "The Universal Passion" he acquired no vulgar fortune—more than three thousand pounds. A considerable sum had already been swallowed up in the South Sea. For this loss he took the vengeance of an author. His Muse makes poetical use more than once of a South Sea Dream.

It is related by Mr. Spence, in his "Manuscript Anecdotes," on the authority of Mr. Rawlinson, that Young, upon the publication of his "Universal Passion," received from the Duke of Grafton two thousand pounds; and that, when one of his friends exclaimed, "Two thousand pounds for a poem!" he said it was the best bargain he ever made in his life, for the poem was worth four thousand. This story may be true; but it seems to have been raised from the two answers of Lord Burghley and Sir Philip Sidney in Spenser's Life.

After inscribing his Satires, not perhaps without the hopes of preferments and honours, to such names as the Duke of Dorset, Mr. Dodington, Mr. Spencer Compton, Lady Elizabeth Germain, and Sir Robert Walpole, he returns to plain panegyric. In 1726 he addressed a poem to Sir Robert Walpole, of which the title sufficiently explains the intention. If Young must be acknowledged a ready celebrator, he did not endeavour, or did not choose, to be a lasting one. "The Instalment" is among the pieces he did not admit into the number of his EXCUSABLE WRITINGS. Yet it contains a couplet which pretends to pant after the power of bestowing immortality:—

"Oh! how I long, enkindled by the theme,
    In deep eternity to launch thy name!"

The bounty of the former reign seems to have been continued, possibly increased, in this. Whatever it might have been, the poet thought he deserved it; for he was not ashamed to acknowledge what, without his acknowledgment, would now perhaps never have been known:—

"My breast, O Walpole, glows with grateful fire.
    The streams of royal bounty, turned by thee,
    Refresh the dry remains of poesy."

If the purity of modern patriotism will term Young a pensioner, it must at least be confessed he was a grateful one.

The reign of the new monarch was ushered in by Young with "Ocean, an Ode." The hint of it was taken from the royal speech, which recommended the increase and the encouragement of the seamen; that they might be "invited, rather than compelled by force and violence, to enter into the service of their country"—a plan which humanity must lament that policy has not even yet been able, or willing, to carry into execution. Prefixed to the original publication were an "Ode to the King, Pater Patriae," and an "Essay on Lyric Poetry." It is but justice to confess that he preserved neither of them; and that the Ode itself, which in the first edition, and in the last, consists of seventy–three stanzas, in the author's own edition is reduced to forty–nine. Among the omitted passages is a "Wish," that concluded the poem, which few would have suspected Young of forming; and of which few, after having formed it, would confess something like their shame by suppression. It stood originally so high in the author's opinion, that he entitled the poem, "Ocean, an Ode. Concluding with a Wish." This wish consists of thirteen stanzas. The first runs thus:—

"O may I STEAL
    Along the VALE
Of humble life, secure from foes!
    My friend sincere,
    My judgment clear,
And gentle business my repose!"

81

Lives of the Poets

The three last stanzas are not more remarkable for just rhymes; but, altogether, they will make rather a curious page in the life of Young:—

"Prophetic schemes,
  And golden dreams,
May I, unsanguine, cast away!
  Have what I HAVE,
  And live, not LEAVE,
Enamoured of the present day!

"My hours my own!
  My faults unknown!
My chief revenue in content!
  Then leave one BEAM
  Of honest FAME!
And scorn the laboured monument!

"Unhurt my urn
  Till that great TURN
When mighty Nature's self shall die,
  Time cease to glide,
  With human pride,
Sunk in the ocean of eternity!"

It is whimsical that he, who was soon to bid adieu to rhyme, should fix upon a measure in which rhyme abounds even to satiety. Of this he said, in his "Essay on Lyric Poetry," prefixed to the poem—" For the more harmony likewise I chose the frequent return of rhyme, which laid me under great difficulties. But difficulties overcome give grace and pleasure. Nor can I account for the PLEASURE OF RHYME IN GENERAL (of which the moderns are too fond) but from this truth." Yet the moderns surely deserve not much censure for their fondness of what, by their own confession, affords pleasure, and abounds in harmony. The next paragraph in his Essay did not occur to him when he talked of "that great turn" in the stanza just quoted. "But then the writer must take care that the difficulty is overcome. That is, he must make rhyme consistent with as perfect sense and expression as could be expected if he was perfectly free from that shackle." Another part of this Essay will convict the following stanza of what every reader will discover in it "involuntary burlesque:—

> "The northern blast,
>   The shattered mast,
> The syrt, the whirlpool, and the rock,
>   The breaking spout,
>   The STARS GONE OUT,
> The boiling strait, the monster's shock."

But would the English poets fill quite so many volumes if all their productions were to be tried, like this, by an elaborate essay on each particular species of poetry of which they exhibit specimens?

If Young be not a lyric poet, he is at least a critic in that sort of poetry; and, if his lyric poetry can be proved bad, it was first proved so by his own criticism. This surely is candid.

Milbourne was styled by Pope "the fairest of critics," only because he exhibited his own version of "Virgil" to be compared with Dryden's, which he condemned, and with which every reader had it not otherwise in his power to compare it. Young was surely not the most unfair of poets for prefixing to a lyric composition an "Essay on Lyric Poetry," so just and impartial as to condemn himself.

We shall soon come to a work, before which we find indeed no critical essay, but which disdains to shrink from the touchstone of the severest critic; and which certainly, as I remember to have heard you say, if it contains some of the worst, contains also some of the best things in the language.

Soon after the appearance of "Ocean," when he was almost fifty, Young entered into orders. In April, 1728, not long after he had put on the gown, he was appointed chaplain to George II.

The tragedy of The Brothers, which was already in rehearsal, he immediately withdrew from the stage. The managers resigned it with some reluctance to the delicacy of the new clergyman. The Epilogue to The Brothers, the only appendages to any of his three plays which he added himself, is, I believe, the only one of the kind. He calls it an historical

Epilogue. Finding that "Guilt's dreadful close his narrow scene denied," he, in a manner, continues the tragedy in the Epilogue, and relates how Rome revenged the shade of Demetrius, and punished Perseus "for this night's deed."

Of Young's taking orders something is told by the biographer of Pope, which places the easiness and simplicity of the poet in a singular light. When he determined on the Church he did not address himself to Sherlock, to Atterbury, or to Hare, for the best instructions in theology, but to Pope, who, in a youthful frolic, advised the diligent perusal of Thomas Aquinas. With this treasure Young retired from interruption to an obscure place in the suburbs. His poetical guide to godliness hearing nothing of him during half a year, and apprehending he might have carried the jest too far, sought after him, and found him just in time to prevent what Ruffhead calls "an irretrievable derangement."

That attachment to his favourite study, which made him think a poet the surest guide to his new profession left him little doubt whether poetry was the surest path to its honours and preferments. Not long indeed after he took orders he published in prose (1728) "A True Estimate of Human Life," dedicated, notwithstanding the Latin quotations with which it abounds, to the Queen; and a sermon preached before the House of Commons, 1729, on the martyrdom of King Charles, entitled, "An Apology for Princes; or, the Reverence due to Government." But the "Second Course," the counterpart of his "Estimate," without which it cannot be called "A True Estimate," though in 1728 it was announced as "soon to be published," never appeared, and his old friends the Muses were not forgotten. In 1730 he relapsed to poetry, and sent into the world "Imperium Pelagi: a Naval Lyric, written in imitation of Pindar's Spirit, occasioned by his Majesty's return from Hanover, September, 1729, and the succeeding peace." It is inscribed to the Duke of Chandos. In the Preface we are told that the Ode is the most spirited kind of poetry, and that the Pindaric is the most spirited kind of Ode. "This I speak," he adds, "with sufficient candour at my own very great peril. But truth has an eternal title to our confession, though we are sure to suffer by it." Behold, again, the fairest of poets. Young's "Imperium Pelagi" was ridiculed in Fielding's "Tom Thumb;" but let us not forget that it was one of his pieces which the author of the "Night Thoughts" deliberately refused to own. Not long after this Pindaric attempt he published two Epistles to Pope, "Concerning the Authors of the Age," 1730. Of these poems one occasion seems to have been an apprehension lest, from the liveliness of his satires, he should not be deemed sufficiently serious for promotion in the Church.

In July, 1730, he was presented by his College to the Rectory of Welwyn, in Hertfordshire. In May, 1731, he married Lady Elizabeth Lee, daughter of the Earl of Lichfield, and widow of Colonel Lee. His connection with this lady arose from his father's acquaintance, already mentioned, with Lady Anne Wharton, who was co–heiress of Sir Henry Lee of Ditchley in Oxfordshire. Poetry had lately been taught by Addison to aspire to the arms of nobility, though not with extraordinary happiness. We may naturally conclude that Young now gave himself up in some measure to the comforts of his new connection, and to the expectations of that preferment which he thought due to his poetical talents, or, at least, to the manner in which they had so frequently been exerted.

The next production of his muse was "The Sea–piece," in two odes.

Young enjoys the credit of what is called an "Extempore Epigram on Voltaire," who, when he was in England, ridiculed, in the company of the jealous English poet, Milton's allegory of "Sin and Death:"

"You are so witty, profligate and thin,
At once we think thee Milton, Death, and Sin."

From the following passage in the poetical dedication of his "Sea– piece" to Voltaire it seems that this extemporaneous reproof, if it must be extemporaneous (for what few will now affirm Voltaire to have deserved any reproof), was something longer than a distich, and something more gentle than the distich just quoted.

"No stranger, sir, though born in foreign climes.
On DORSET Downs, when Milton's page,
With Sin and Death provoked thy rage,
Thy rage provoked who soothed with GENTLE rhymes?"

By "Dorset Downs" he probably meant Mr. Dodington's seat. In Pitt's Poems is "An Epistle to Dr. Edward Young, at Eastbury, in Dorsetshire, on the Review at Sarum, 1722."

"While with your Dodington retired you sit,
Charmed with his flowing Burgundy and wit," etc.

Lives of the Poets

Thomson, in his Autumn, addressing Mr. Dodington calls his seat the seat of the Muses,

"Where, in the secret bower and winding walk,
For virtuous Young and thee they twine the bay."

The praises Thomson bestows but a few lines before on Philips, the second

"Who nobly durst, in rhyme—unfettered verse,
With British freedom sing the British song,"

added to Thomson's example and success, might perhaps induce Young, as we shall see presently, to write his great work without rhyme.

In 1734 he published "The Foreign Address, or the best Argument for Peace, occasioned by the British Fleet and the Posture of Affairs. Written in the Character of a Sailor." It is not to be found in the author's four volumes. He now appears to have given up all hopes of overtaking Pindar, and perhaps at last resolved to turn his ambition to some original species of poetry. This poem concludes with a formal farewell to Ode, which few of Young's readers will regret:

"My shell, which Clio gave, which KINGS APPLAUD,
Which Europe's bleeding genius called abroad,
Adieu!"

In a species of poetry altogether his own he next tried his skill, and succeeded.

Of his wife he was deprived in 1741. Lady Elizabeth had lost, after her marriage with Young, an amiable daughter, by her former husband, just after she was married to Mr. Temple, son of Lord Palmerston. Mr. Temple did not long remain after his wife, though he was married a second time to a daughter of Sir John Barnard's, whose son is the present peer. Mr. and Mrs. Temple have generally been considered as Philander and Narcissa. From the great friendship which constantly subsisted between Mr. Temple and Young, as well as from other circumstances, it is probable that the poet had both him and Mrs. Temple in view for these characters; though, at the same time, some passages respecting Philander do not appear to suit either Mr. Temple or any other person with whom Young was known to be connected or acquainted, while all the circumstances relating to Narcissa have been constantly found applicable to Young's daughter–in–law. At what short intervals the poet tells us he was wounded by the deaths of the three persons particularly lamented, none that has read the "Night Thoughts" (and who has not read them?) needs to be informed.

"Insatiate archer! could not one suffice?
Thy shaft flew thrice, and thrice my peace was slain;
And thrice, ere thrice yon moon had filled her horn."

Yet how is it possible that Mr. and Mrs. Temple and Lady Elizabeth Young could be these three victims, over whom Young has hitherto been pitied for having to pour the "Midnight Sorrows" of his religious poetry? Mrs. Temple died in 1736; Mr. Temple four years afterwards, in 1740; and the poet's wife seven months after Mr. Temple, in 1741. How could the insatiate archer thrice slay his peace, in these three persons, "ere thrice the moon had filled her horn." But in the short preface to "The Complaint" he seriously tells us, "that the occasion of this poem was real, not fictitious, and that the facts mentioned did naturally pour these moral reflections on the thought of the writer." It is probable, therefore, that in these three contradictory lines the poet complains more than the father–in–law, the friend, or the widower. Whatever names belong to these facts, or if the names be those generally supposed, whatever heightening a poet's sorrow may have given the facts; to the sorrow Young felt from them religion and morality are indebted for the "Night Thoughts." There is a pleasure sure in sadness which mourners only know! Of these poems the two or three first have been perused perhaps more eagerly and more frequently than the rest. When he got as far as the fourth or fifth his original motive for taking up the pen was answered; his grief was naturally either diminished or exhausted. We still find the same pious poet, but we hear less of Philander and Narcissa, and less of the mourner whom he loved to pity.

Mrs. Temple died of a consumption at Lyons, on her way to Nice, the year after her marriage; that is, when poetry relates the fact, "in her bridal hour." It is more than poetically true that Young accompanied her to the Continent:

"I flew, I snatched her from the rigid North,
And bore her nearer to the sun."

But in vain. Her funeral was attended with the difficulties painted in such animated colours in "Night the Third." After her death the remainder of the party passed the ensuing winter at Nice. The poet seems perhaps in these compositions to dwell with more melancholy on the death of Philander and Narcissa than of his wife. But it is only for this reason. He who runs and reads may remember that in the "Night Thoughts" Philander and Narcissa are often mentioned and often lamented. To recollect lamentations over the author's wife the memory must have been charged with distinct passages. This lady brought him one child, Frederick, now living, to whom the Prince of Wales was godfather.

That domestic grief is, in the first instance, to be thanked for these ornaments to our language it is impossible to deny. Nor would it be common hardiness to contend that worldly discontent had no hand in these joint productions of poetry and piety. Yet am I by no means sure that, at any rate, we should not have had something of the same colour from Young's pencil, notwithstanding the liveliness of his satires. In so long a life causes for discontent and occasions for grief must have occurred. It is not clear to me that his Muse was not sitting upon the watch for the first which happened. "Night Thoughts" were not uncommon to her, even when first she visited the poet, and at a time when he himself was remarkable neither for gravity nor gloominess. In his "Last Day," almost his earliest poem, he calls her "The Melancholy Maid,"

> "whom dismal scenes delight,
> Frequent at tombs and in the realms of Night."

In the prayer which concludes the second book of the same poem, he says:

> "Oh! permit the gloom of solemn night
> To sacred thought may forcibly invite.
> Oh! how divine to tread the milky way,
> To the bright palace of Eternal Day!"

When Young was writing a tragedy, Grafton is said by Spence to have sent him a human skull, with a candle in it, as a lamp, and the poet is reported to have used it. What he calls "The TRUE Estimate of Human Life," which has already been mentioned, exhibits only the wrong side of the tapestry, and being asked why he did not show the right, he is said to have replied that he could not. By others it has been told me that this was finished, but

88

that, before there existed any copy, it was torn in pieces by a lady's monkey. Still, is it altogether fair to dress up the poet for the man, and to bring the gloominess of the "Night Thoughts" to prove the gloominess of Young, and to show that his genius, like the genius of Swift, was in some measure the sullen inspiration of discontent? From them who answer in the affirmative it should not be concealed that, though "Invisibilia non decipiunt" appeared upon a deception in Young's grounds, and "Ambulantes in horto audierunt vocem Dei" on a building in his garden, his parish was indebted to the good humour of the author of the "Night Thoughts" for an assembly and a bowling green.

Whether you think with me, I know not; but the famous "De mortuis nil nisi bonum" always appeared to me to savour more of female weakness than of manly reason. He that has too much feeling to speak ill of the dead, who, if they cannot defend themselves, are at least ignorant of his abuse, will not hesitate by the most wanton calumny to destroy the quiet, the reputation, the fortune of the living. Yet censure is not heard beneath the tomb, any more than praise. "De mortuis nil nisi verum—De vivis nil nisi bonum" would approach much nearer to good sense. After all, the few handfuls of remaining dust which once composed the body of the author of the "Night Thoughts" feel not much concern whether Young pass now for a man of sorrow or for "a fellow of infinite jest." To this favour must come the whole family of Yorick. His immortal part, wherever that now dwells, is still less solicitous on this head. But to a son of worth and sensibility it is of some little consequence whether contemporaries believe, and posterity be taught to believe, that his debauched and reprobate life cast a Stygian gloom over the evening of his father's days, saved him the trouble of feigning a character completely detestable, and succeeded at last in bringing his "grey hairs with sorrow to the grave." The humanity of the world, little satisfied with inventing perhaps a melancholy disposition for the father, proceeds next to invent an argument in support of their invention, and chooses that Lorenzo should be Young's own son. "The Biographia," and every account of Young, pretty roundly assert this to be the fact; of the absolute impossibility of which, the "Biographia" itself, in particular dates, contains undeniable evidence. Readers I know there are of a strange turn of mind, who will hereafter peruse the "Night Thoughts" with less satisfaction; who will wish they had still been deceived; who will quarrel with me for discovering that no such character as their Lorenzo ever yet disgraced human nature or broke a father's heart. Yet would these admirers of the sublime and terrible be offended should you set them down for cruel and for savage? Of this report, inhuman to the surviving son, if it be true, in proportion as the character of Lorenzo is diabolical, where are we to find the proof? Perhaps it is clear from the poems.

From the first line to the last of the "Night Thoughts" no one expression can be discovered which betrays anything like the father. In the "Second Night" I find an expression which betrays something else—that Lorenzo was his friend; one, it is possible, of his former companions; one of the Duke of Wharton's set. The poet styles him "gay friend;" an appellation not very natural from a pious incensed father to such a being as he paints Lorenzo, and that being his son. But let us see how he has sketched this dreadful portrait, from the sight of some of whose features the artist himself must have turned away with horror. A subject more shocking, if his only child really sat to him, than the crucifixion of Michael Angelo; upon the horrid story told of which Young composed a short poem of fourteen lines in the early part of his life, which he did not think deserved to be republished. In the "First Night" the address to the poet's supposed son is:—

"Lorenzo, Fortune makes her court to thee."

In the "Fifth Night:"—

"And burns Lorenzo still for the sublime
 Of life? to hang his airy nest on high?"

Is this a picture of the son of the Rector of Welwyn? "Eighth Night:"—

"In foreign realms (for thou hast travelled far)"—

which even now does not apply to his son. In "Night Five:"—

"So wept Lorenzo fair Clarissa's fate,
 Who gave that angel–boy on whom he dotes,
 And died to give him, orphaned in his birth!"

At the beginning of the "Fifth Night" we find:—

"Lorenzo, to recriminate is just,
 I grant the man is vain who writes for praise."

But, to cut short all inquiry; if any one of these passages, if any passage in the poems, be applicable, my friend shall pass for Lorenzo. The son of the author of the "Night

Thoughts" was not old enough, when they were written, to recriminate or to be a father. The "Night Thoughts" were begun immediately after the mournful event of 1741. The first "Nights" appear, in the books of the Company of Stationers, as the property of Robert Dodsley, in 1742. The Preface to "Night Seven" is dated July 7th, 1744. The marriage, in consequence of which the supposed Lorenzo was born, happened in May, 1731. Young's child was not born till June, 1733. In 1741, this Lorenzo, this finished infidel, this father to whose education Vice had for some years put the last hand, was only eight years old. An anecdote of this cruel sort, so open to contradiction, so impossible to be true, who could propagate? Thus easily are blasted the reputation of the living and of the dead. "Who, then, was Lorenzo?" exclaim the readers I have mentioned. If we cannot be sure that he was his son, which would have been finely terrible, was he not his nephew, his cousin? These are questions which I do not pretend to answer. For the sake of human nature, I could wish Lorenzo to have been only the creation of the poet's fancy: like the Quintus of Anti Lucretius, "quo nomine," says Polignac, "quemvis Atheum intellige." That this was the case many expressions in the "Night Thoughts" would seem to prove, did not a passage in "Night Eight" appear to show that he had somebody in his eye for the groundwork at least of the painting. Lovelace or Lorenzo may be feigned characters; but a writer does not feign a name of which he only gives the initial letter:—

"Tell not Calista. She will laugh thee dead,
Or send thee to her hermitage with L——."

The "Biographia," not satisfied with pointing out the son of Young, in that son's lifetime, as his father's Lorenzo, travels out of its way into the history of the son, and tells of his having been forbidden his college at Oxford for misbehaviour. How such anecdotes, were they true, tend to illustrate the life of Young, it is not easy to discover. Was the son of the author of the "Night Thoughts," indeed, forbidden his college for a time, at one of our Universities? The author of "Paradise Lost" is by some supposed to have been disgracefully ejected from the other. From juvenile follies who is free? But, whatever the "Biographia" chooses to relate, the son of Young experienced no dismission from his college, either lasting or temporary. Yet, were nature to indulge him with a second youth, and to leave him at the same time the experience of that which is past, he would probably spend it differently—who would not?—he would certainly be the occasion of less uneasiness to his father. But, from the same experience, he would as certainly, in the same case, be treated differently by his father.

Lives of the Poets

Young was a poet: poets, with reverence be it spoken, do not make the best parents. Fancy and imagination seldom deign to stoop from their heights; always stoop unwillingly to the low level of common duties. Aloof from vulgar life, they pursue their rapid flight beyond the ken of mortals, and descend not to earth but when compelled by necessity. The prose of ordinary occurrences is beneath the dignity of poets. He who is connected with the author of the "Night Thoughts" only by veneration for the Poet and the Christian may be allowed to observe that Young is one of those concerning whom, as you remark in your account of Addison, it is proper rather to say "nothing that is false than all that is true." But the son of Young would almost sooner, I know, pass for a Lorenzo than see himself vindicated, at the expense of his father's memory, from follies which, if it may be thought blameable in a boy to have committed them, it is surely praiseworthy in a man to lament and certainly not only unnecessary, but cruel in a biographer to record.

Of the "Night Thoughts," notwithstanding their author's professed retirement, all are inscribed to great or to growing names. He had not yet weaned himself from earls and dukes, from the Speakers of the House of Commons, Lords Commissioners of the Treasury, and Chancellors of the Exchequer. In "Night Eight" the politician plainly betrays himself:—

"Think no post needful that demands a knave:
When late our civil helm was shifting hands,
So P—— thought: think better if you can."

Yet it must be confessed that at the conclusion of "Night Nine," weary perhaps of courting earthly patrons, he tells his soul—

"Henceforth
Thy PATRON he, whose diadem has dropped
You gems of Heaven; Eternity thy prize;
And leave the racers of the world their own."

The "Fourth Night" was addressed by "a much-indebted Muse" to the Honourable Mr. Yorke, now Lord Hardwicke, who meant to have laid the Muse under still greater obligation, by the living of Shenfield, in Essex, if it had become vacant. The "First Night" concludes with this passage:—

"Dark, though not blind, like thee, Meonides;
Or, Milton, thee. Ah! could I reach your strain;
Or his who made Meonides our own!
Man too he sung. Immortal man I sing.
Oh had he pressed his theme, pursued the track
Which opens out of darkness into day!
Oh, had he mounted on his wing of fire,
Soared, where I sink, and sung immortal man—
How had it blest mankind, and rescued me!"

To the author of these lines was dedicated, in 1756, the first volume of an "Essay on the Writings and Genius of Pope," which attempted, whether justly or not, to pluck from Pope his "Wing of Fire," and to reduce him to a rank at least one degree lower than the first class of English poets. If Young accepted and approved the dedication, he countenanced this attack upon the fame of him whom he invokes as his Muse.

Part of "paper–sparing" Pope's Third Book of the "Odyssey," deposited in the Museum, is written upon the back of a letter signed "E. Young," which is clearly the handwriting of our Young. The letter, dated only May 2nd, seems obscure; but there can be little doubt that the friendship he requests was a literary one, and that he had the highest literary opinion of Pope. The request was a prologue, I am told.

"May the 2nd.

"DEAR SIR;—Having been often from home, I know not if you have done me the favour of calling on me. But, be that as it will, I much want that instance of your friendship I mentioned in my last; a friendship I am very sensible I can receive from no one but yourself. I should not urge this thing so much but for very particular reasons; nor can you be at a loss to conceive how a 'trifle of this nature' may be of serious moment to me; and while I am in hopes of the great advantage of your advice about it, I shall not be so absurd as to make any further step without it. I know you are much engaged, and only hope to hear of you at your entire leisure.
"I am, sir, your most faithful
"and obedient servant,
"E. YOUNG."

Lives of the Poets

Nay, even after Pope's death, he says in "Night Seven:"—

"Pope, who could'st make immortals, art thou dead?"

Either the "Essay," then, was dedicated to a patron who disapproved its doctrine, which I have been told by the author was not the case; or Young appears, in his old age, to have bartered for a dedication an opinion entertained of his friend through all that part of life when he must have been best able to form opinions. From this account of Young, two or three short passages, which stand almost together in "Night Four," should not be excluded. They afford a picture, by his own hand, from the study of which my readers may choose to form their own opinion of the features of his mind and the complexion of his life.

> "Ah me! the dire effect
> Of loitering here, of death defrauded long;
> Of old so gracious (and let that suffice),
> MY VERY MASTER KNOWS ME NOT.
> I've been so long remembered I'm forgot.
>   * *
> When in his courtiers' ears I pour my plaint,
> They drink it as the Nectar of the Great;
> And squeeze my hand, and beg me come to–morrow.
>   * *
> Twice told the period spent on stubborn Troy,
> Court favour, yet untaken, I BESIEGE.
>   * *
> If this song lives, Posterity shall know
> One, though in Britain born, with courtiers bred,
> Who thought, even gold might come a day too late;
> Nor on his subtle deathbed planned his scheme
> For future vacancies in Church or State."

Deduct from the writer's age "twice told the period spent on stubborn Troy," and you will still leave him more than forty when he sate down to the miserable siege of court–favour. He has before told us—

Lives of the Poets

"A fool at forty is a fool indeed."

After all, the siege seems to have been raised only in consequence of what the general thought his "deathbed." By these extraordinary poems, written after he was sixty, of which I have been led to say so much, I hope, by the wish of doing justice to the living and the dead, it was the desire of Young to be principally known. He entitled the four volumes which he published himself, "The Works of the Author of the Night Thoughts." While it is remembered that from these he excluded many of his writings, let it not be forgotten that the rejected pieces contained nothing prejudicial to the cause of virtue or of religion. Were everything that Young ever wrote to be published, he would only appear perhaps in a less respectable light as a poet, and more despicable as a dedicator; he would not pass for a worse Christian or for a worse man. This enviable praise is due to Young. Can it be claimed by every writer? His dedications, after all, he had perhaps no right to suppress. They all, I believe, speak, not a little to the credit of his gratitude, of favours received; and I know not whether the author, who has once solemnly printed an acknowledgment of a favour, should not always print it. Is it to the credit or to the discredit of Young, as a poet, that of his "Night Thoughts" the French are particularly fond?

Of the "Epitaph on Lord Aubrey Beauclerk," dated 1740, all I know is, that I find it in the late body of English poetry, and that I am sorry to find it there. Notwithstanding the farewell which he seemed to have taken in the "Night Thoughts" of everything which bore the least resemblance to ambition, he dipped again in politics. In 1745 he wrote "Reflections on the Public Situation of the Kingdom, addressed to the Duke of Newcastle;" indignant, as it appears, to behold

> "——a pope–bred Princeling crawl ashore,
> And whistle cut–throats, with those swords that scraped
> Their barren rocks for wretched sustenance,
> To cut his passage to the British throne."

This political poem might be called a "Night Thought;" indeed, it was originally printed as the conclusion of the "Night Thoughts," though he did not gather it with his other works.

Lives of the Poets

Prefixed to the second edition of Howe's "Devout Meditations" is a letter from Young, dated January 19, 1752, addressed to Archibald Macauly, Esq., thanking him for the book, "which," he says, "he shall never lay far out of his reach; for a greater demonstration of a sound head and a sincere heart he never saw."

In 1753, when The Brothers had lain by him above thirty years, it appeared upon the stage. If any part of his fortune had been acquired by servility of adulation, he now determined to deduct from it no inconsiderable sum, as a gift to the Society for the Propagation of the Gospel. To this sum he hoped the profits of The Brothers would amount. In his calculation he was deceived; but by the bad success of his play the Society was not a loser. The author made up the sum he originally intended, which was a thousand pounds, from his own pocket.

The next performance which he printed was a prose publication, entitled "The Centaur Not Fabulous, in Six Letters to a Friend on the Life in Vogue." The conclusion is dated November 29, 1754. In the third letter is described the death-bed of the "gay, young, noble, ingenious, accomplished, and most wretched Altamont." His last words were—"My principles have poisoned my friend, my extravagance has beggared my boy, my unkindness has murdered my wife!" Either Altamont and Lorenzo were the twin production of fancy, or Young was unlucky enough to know two characters who bore no little resemblance to each other in perfection of wickedness. Report has been accustomed to call Altamont Lord Euston.

"The Old Man's Relapse," occasioned by an Epistle to Walpole, if written by Young, which I much doubt, must have been written very late in life. It has been seen, I am told, in a Miscellany published thirty years before his death. In 1758 he exhibited "The Old Man's Relapse," in more than words, by again becoming a dedicator, and publishing a sermon addressed to the king.

The lively letter in prose, on "Original Composition," addressed to Richardson, the author of "Clarissa," appeared in 1759. Though he despairs "of breaking through the frozen obstructions of age and care's incumbent cloud into that flow of thought and brightness of expression which subjects so polite require," yet it is more like the production of untamed, unbridled youth, than of jaded fourscore. Some sevenfold volumes put him in mind of Ovid's sevenfold channels of the Nile at the conflagration:—

Lives of the Poets

"—ostia septem
Pulverulenta vocant, septem sine flumine valles."

Such leaden labours are like Lycurgus's iron money, which was so much less in value than in bulk, that it required barns for strong boxes, and a yoke of oxen to draw five hundred pounds. If there is a famine of invention in the land, we must travel, he says, like Joseph's brethren, far for food, we must visit the remote and rich ancients. But an inventive genius may safely stay at home; that, like the widow's cruse, is divinely replenished from within, and affords us a miraculous delight. He asks why it should seem altogether impossible that Heaven's latest editions of the human mind may be the most correct and fair? And Jonson, he tells us, was very learned, as Samson was very strong, to his own hurt. Blind to the nature of tragedy, he pulled down all antiquity on his head, and buried himself under it. Is this "care's incumbent cloud," or "the frozen obstructions of age?" In this letter Pope is severely censured for his "fall from Homer's numbers, free as air, lofty and harmonious as the spheres, into childish shackles and tinkling sounds; for putting Achilles into petticoats a second time:" but we are told that the dying swan talked over an epic plan with Young a few weeks before his decease. Young's chief inducement to write this letter was, as he confesses, that he might erect a monumental marble to the memory of an old friend. He, who employed his pious pen for almost the last time in thus doing justice to the exemplary death–bed of Addison, might probably, at the close of his own life, afford no unuseful lesson for the deaths of others. In the postscript he writes to Richardson that he will see in his next how far Addison is an original. But no other letter appears.

The few lines which stand in the last edition, as "sent by Lord Melcombe to Dr. Young not long before his lordship's death," were indeed so sent, but were only an introduction to what was there meant by "The Muse's Latest Spark." The poem is necessary, whatever may be its merit, since the Preface to it is already printed. Lord Melcombe called his Tusculum "La Trappe":—

"Love thy country, wish it well,
  Not with too intense a care;
'Tis enough, that, when it fell,
  Thou its ruin didst not share.

Lives of the Poets

Envy's censure, Flattery's praise,
  With unmoved indifference view;
Learn to tread life's dangerous maze,
  With unerring Virtue's clue.

Void of strong desire and fear,
  Life's void ocean trust no more;
Strive thy little bark to steer
  With the tide, but near the shore.

Thus prepared, thy shortened sail
  Shall, whene'er the winds increase,
Seizing each propitious gale,
  Waft thee to the Port of Peace.

Keep thy conscience from offence,
  And tempestuous passions free,
So, when thou art called from hence,
  Easy shall thy passage be;

Easy shall thy passage be,
  Cheerful thy allotted stay,
Short the account 'twixt God and thee;
  Hope shall meet thee on the way:

Truth shall lead thee to the gate,
  Mercy's self shall let thee in,
Where its never–changing state,
  Full perfection, shall begin."

The poem was accompanied by a letter.

"La Trappe, the 27th of October, 1761 "DEAR SIR,—You seemed to like the
ode I sent you for your amusement; I now send it you as a present. If you please to accept
of it, and are willing that our friendship should be known when we are gone, you will be
pleased to leave this among those of your own papers that may possibly see the light by a

posthumous publication. God send us health while we stay, and an easy journey!—My dear Dr. Young,

>"Yours, most cordially,
>"MELCOMBE."

In 1762, a short time before his death, Young published "Resignation." Notwithstanding the manner in which it was really forced from him by the world, criticism has treated it with no common severity. If it shall be thought not to deserve the highest praise, on the other side of fourscore, by whom, except by Newton and by Waller, has praise been merited?

To Mrs. Montagu, the famous champion of Shakespeare, I am indebted for the history of "Resignation." Observing that Mrs. Boscawen, in the midst of her grief for the loss of the admiral, derived consolation from the perusal of the "Night Thoughts," Mrs. Montagu proposed a visit to the author. From conversing with Young, Mrs. Boscawen derived still further consolation; and to that visit she and the world were indebted for this poem. It compliments Mrs. Montagu in the following lines:—

>"Yet write I must. A lady sues:
> How shameful her request!
>My brain in labour with dull rhyme,
> Hers teeming with the best!"

And again—

>"A friend you have, and I the same,
> Whose prudent, soft address
>Will bring to life those healing thoughts
> Which died in your distress.
>That friend, the spirit of my theme
> Extracting for your ease,
>Will leave to me the dreg, in thoughts
> Too common; such as these."

By the same lady I was enabled to say, in her own words, that Young's unbounded genius appeared to greater advantage in the companion than even in the author; that the Christian was in him a character still more inspired, more enraptured, more sublime, than the poet; and that, in his ordinary conversation—

"—letting down the golden chain from high,
He drew his audience upward to the sky."

Notwithstanding Young had said, in his "Conjectures on Original Composition," that "blank verse is verse unfallen, uncursed—verse reclaimed, re-enthroned in the true language of the gods;" notwithstanding he administered consolation to his own grief in this immortal language, Mrs. Boscawen was comforted in rhyme.

While the poet and the Christian were applying this comfort, Young had himself occasion for comfort, in consequence of the sudden death of Richardson, who was printing the former part of the poem. Of Richardson's death he says—

"When heaven would kindly set us free,
And earth's enchantment end;
It takes the most effectual means,
And robs us of a friend."

To "Resignation" was prefixed an apology for its appearance, to which more credit is due than to the generality of such apologies, from Young's unusual anxiety that no more productions of his old age should disgrace his former fame. In his will, dated February, 1760, he desires of his executors, IN A PARTICULAR MANNER, that all his manuscript books and writings, whatever, might be burned, except his book of accounts. In September, 1764, he added a kind of codicil, wherein he made it his dying entreaty to his housekeeper, to whom he left 1,000 pounds, "that all his manuscripts might be destroyed as soon as he was dead, which would greatly oblige her deceased FRIEND."

It may teach mankind the uncertainty of wordly friendships to know that Young, either by surviving those he loved, or by outliving their affections, could only recollect the names of two FRIENDS, his housekeeper and a hatter, to mention in his will; and it may serve to repress that testamentary pride, which too often seeks for sounding names and titles, to be informed that the author of the "Night Thoughts" did not blush to leave a legacy to his "friend Henry Stevens, a hatter at the Temple-gate." Of these two remaining friends, one went before Young. But, at eighty-four, "where," as he asks in The Centaur, "is that world into which we were born?" The same humility which marked a hatter and a housekeeper for the friends of the author of the "Night Thoughts," had before bestowed the same title on his footman, in an epitaph in his "Churchyard" upon James Baker, dated 1749; which I am glad to find in the late collection of his works. Young and his housekeeper were ridiculed, with more ill-nature than wit, in a kind of novel published by Kidgell in 1755, called "The Card," under the names of Dr. Elwes and Mrs. Fusby. In April, 1765, at an age to which few attain, a period was put to the life of Young. He had performed no duty for three or four years, but he retained his intellects to the last.

Much is told in the "Biographia," which I know not to have been true, of the manner of his burial; of the master and children of a charity-school, which he founded in his parish, who neglected to attend their benefactor's corpse; and a bell which was not caused to toll as often as upon those occasions bells usually toll. Had that humanity, which is here lavished upon things of little consequence either to the living or to the dead, been shown in its proper place to the living, I should have had less to say about Lorenzo. They who lament that these misfortunes happened to Young, forget the praise he bestows upon Socrates, in the Preface to "Night Seven," for resenting his friend's request about his funeral. During some part of his life Young was abroad, but I have not been able to learn any particulars. In his seventh Satire he says,

"When, after battle, I the field have SEEN
Spread o'er with ghastly shapes which once were men."

It is known, also, that from this or from some other field he once wandered into the camp with a classic in his hand, which he was reading intently; and had some difficulty to prove that he was only an absent poet, and not a spy.

The curious reader of Young's life will naturally inquire to what it was owing, that though he lived almost forty years after he took orders, which included one whole reign uncommonly long, and part of another, he was never thought worthy of the least preferment. The author of the "Night Thoughts" ended his days upon a living which came to him from his college without any favour, and to which he probably had an eye when he determined on the Church. To satisfy curiosity of this kind is, at this distance of time, far from easy. The parties themselves know not often, at the instant, why they are neglected, or why they are preferred. The neglect of Young is by some ascribed to his having attached himself to the Prince of Wales, and to his having preached an offensive sermon at St. James's. It has been told me that he had two hundred a year in the late reign, by the patronage of Walpole; and that, whenever any one reminded the king of Young, the only answer was, "he has a pension." All the light thrown on this inquiry, by the following letter from Secker, only serves to show at what a late period of life the author of the "Night Thoughts" solicited preferment:—

"Deanery of St. Paul's, July 8, 1758.

"GOOD DR. YOUNG,—I have long wondered that more suitable notice of your great merit hath not been taken by persons in power. But how to remedy the omission I see not. No encouragement hath ever been given me to mention things of this nature to his majesty. And therefore, in all likelihood, the only consequence of doing it would be weakening the little influence which else I may possibly have on some other occasions. Your fortune and your reputation set you above the need of advancement; and your sentiments, above that concern for it, on your own account, which, on that of the public, is sincerely felt by
"Your loving Brother, THO. CANT."

At last, at the age of fourscore, he was appointed, in 1761, Clerk of the Closet to the Princess Dowager. One obstacle must have stood not a little in the way of that preferment after which his whole life seems to have panted. Though he took orders, he never entirely shook off politics. He was always the lion of his master Milton, "pawing to get free his hinder parts." By this conduct, if he gained some friends, he made many enemies. Again: Young was a poet; and again, with reverence be it spoken, poets by profession do not always make the best clergymen. If the author of the "Night Thoughts" composed many sermons, he did not oblige the public with many. Besides, in the latter part of his life, Young was fond of holding himself out for a man retired from the world. But he seemed to have forgotten that the same verse which contains "oblitus meorum," contains also "obliviscendus et illis." The brittle chain of worldly friendship and patronage is broken as effectually, when one goes beyond the length of it, as when the other does. To the vessel which is sailing from the shore, it only appears that the shore also recedes; in life it is truly thus. He who retires from the world will find himself, in reality, deserted as fast, if not faster, by the world. The public is not to be treated as the coxcomb treats his mistress; to be threatened with desertion, in order to increase fondness.

Lives of the Poets

Young seems to have been taken at his word. Notwithstanding his frequent complaints of being neglected, no hand was reached out to pull him from that retirement of which he declared himself enamoured. Alexander assigned no palace for the residence of Diogenes, who boasted his surly satisfaction with his tub. Of the domestic manners and petty habits of the author of the "Night Thoughts," I hoped to have given you an account from the best authority; but who shall dare to say, To—morrow I will be wise or virtuous, or to—morrow I will do a particular thing? Upon inquiring for his housekeeper, I learned that she was buried two days before I reached the town of her abode.

In a letter from Tscharner, a noble foreigner, to Count Haller, Tscharner says, he has lately spent four days with Young at Welwyn, where the author tastes all the ease and pleasure mankind can desire. "Everything about him shows the man, each individual being placed by rule. All is neat without art. He is very pleasant in conversation, and extremely polite." This, and more, may possibly be true; but Tscharner's was a first visit, a visit of curiosity and admiration, and a visit which the author expected.

Of Edward Young an anecdote which wanders among readers is not true, that he was Fielding's Parson Adams. The original of that famous painting was William Young, who was a clergyman. He supported an uncomfortable existence by translating for the booksellers from Greek, and, if he did not seem to be his own friend, was at least no man's enemy. Yet the facility with which this report has gained belief in the world argues, were it not sufficiently known that the author of the "Night Thoughts" bore some resemblance to Adams. The attention which Young bestowed upon the perusal of books is not unworthy imitation. When any passage pleased him he appears to have folded down the leaf. On these passages he bestowed a second reading. But the labours of man are too frequently vain. Before he returned to much of what he had once approved he died. Many of his books, which I have seen, are by those notes of approbation so swelled beyond their real bulk, that they will hardly shut.

"What though we wade in wealth, or soar in fame!
Earth's highest station ends in HERE HE LIES!
And DUST TO DUST concludes her noblest song!"

The author of these lines is not without his 'Hic jacet.' By the good sense of his son it contains none of that praise which no marble can make the bad or the foolish merit; which, without the direction of stone or a turf, will find its way, sooner or later, to the deserving.

> M. S.
> Optimi parentis
> EDWARDI YOUNG, LL.D. Hujus Ecclesiae rect. et Elizabethae faem. praenob
> Conjugis ejus amantissimae
> Pio et gratissimo animo hoc marmor posuit
> F. Y.
> Filius superstes.

Is it not strange that the author of the "Night Thoughts" has inscribed no monument to the memory of his lamented wife? Yet what marble will endure as long as the poems?

Such, my good friend, is the account which I have been able to collect of the great Young. That it may be long before anything like what I have just transcribed be necessary for you, is the sincere wish of,
> Dear Sir, your greatly obliged Friend,
> HERBERT CROFT, Jun.
Lincoln's Inn, Sept., 1780.

P.S.—This account of Young was seen by you in manuscript, you know, sir, and, though I could not prevail on you to make any alteration, you insisted on striking out one passage, because it said that if I did not wish you to live long for your sake, I did for the sake of myself and of the world. But this postscript you will not see before the printing of it, and I will say here, in spite of you, how I feel myself honoured and bettered by your friendship, and that if I do credit to the Church, after which I always longed, and for which I am now going to give in exchange the bar, though not at so late a period of life as Young took orders, it will be owing, in no small measure, to my having had the happiness of calling the author of "The Rambler" my friend. H. C.
Oxford, Oct., 1782.

Of Young's Poems it is difficult to give any general character, for he has no uniformity of manner; one of his pieces has no great resemblance to another. He began to write early and continued long, and at different times had different modes of poetical excellence in view. His numbers are sometimes smooth and sometimes rugged; his style is sometimes concatenated and sometimes abrupt, sometimes diffusive and sometimes concise. His plan seems to have started in his mind at the present moment, and his thoughts appear the effect of chance, sometimes adverse and sometimes lucky, with very little operation of judgment. He was not one of those writers whom experience improves, and who, observing their own faults, become gradually correct. His poem on the "Last Day," his first great performance, has an equability and propriety, which he afterwards either never endeavoured or never attained. Many paragraphs are noble, and few are mean, yet the whole is languid; the plan is too much extended, and a succession of images divides and weakens the general conception, but the great reason why the reader is disappointed is that the thought of the LAST DAY makes every man more than poetical by spreading over his mind a general obscurity of sacred horror, that oppresses distinction and disdains expression. His story of "Jane Grey" was never popular. It is written with elegance enough, but Jane is too heroic to be pitied.

"The Universal Passion" is indeed a very great performance. It is said to be a series of epigrams, but, if it be, it is what the author intended; his endeavour was at the production of striking distichs and pointed sentences, and his distichs have the weight of solid sentiments, and his points the sharpness of resistless truth. His characters are often selected with discernment and drawn with nicety; his illustrations are often happy, and his reflections often just. His species of satire is between those of Horace and Juvenal, and he has the gaiety of Horace without his laxity of numbers, and the morality of Juvenal with greater variation of images. He plays, indeed, only on the surface of life; he never penetrates the recesses of the mind, and therefore the whole power of his poetry is exhausted by a single perusal; his conceits please only when they surprise. To translate he never condescended, unless his "Paraphrase on Job" may be considered as a version, in which he has not, I think, been unsuccessful; he indeed favoured himself by choosing those parts which most easily admit the ornaments of English poetry. He had least success in his lyric attempts, in which he seems to have been under some malignant influence; he is always labouring to be great, and at last is only turgid.

In his "Night Thoughts" he has exhibited a very wide display of original poetry, variegated with deep reflections and striking allusions, a wilderness of thought, in which the fertility of fancy scatters flowers of every hue and of every odour. This is one of the few poems in which blank verse could not be changed for rhyme but with disadvantage. The wild diffusion of the sentiments and the digressive sallies of imagination would have been compressed and restrained by confinement to rhyme. The excellence of this work is not exactness but copiousness; particular lines are not to be regarded; the power is in the whole, and in the whole there is a magnificence like that ascribed to Chinese plantation, the magnificence of vast extent and endless diversity.

His last poem was the "Resignation," in which he made, as he was accustomed, an experiment of a new mode of writing, and succeeded better than in his "Ocean" or his "Merchant." It was very falsely represented as a proof of decaying faculties. There is Young in every stanza, such as he often was in the highest vigour. His tragedies, not making part of the collection, I had forgotten, till Mr. Stevens recalled them to my thoughts, by remarking, that he seemed to have one favourite catastrophe, as his three plays all concluded with lavish suicide, a method by which, as Dryden remarked, a poet easily rids his scene of persons whom he wants not to keep alive. In Busiris there are the greatest ebullitions of imagination, but the pride of Busiris is such as no other man can have, and the whole is too remote from known life to raise either grief, terror, or indignation. The Revenge approaches much nearer to human practices and manners, and therefore keeps possession of the stage; the first design seems suggested by Othello, but the reflections, the incidents, and the diction, are original. The moral observations are so introduced and so expressed as to have all the novelty that can be required. Of The Brothers I may be allowed to say nothing, since nothing was ever said of it by the public. It must be allowed of Young's poetry that it abounds in thought, but without much accuracy or selection. When he lays hold of an illustration he pursues it beyond expectation, sometimes happily, as in his parallel of Quicksilver with Pleasure, which I have heard repeated with approbation by a lady, of whose praise he would have been justly proud, and which is very ingenious, very subtle, and almost exact; but sometimes he is less lucky, as when, in his "Night Thoughts," having it dropped into his mind that the orbs, floating in space, might be called the CLUSTER of creation, he thinks of a cluster of grapes, and says, that they all hang on the great vine, drinking the "nectareous juice of immortal life." His conceits are sometimes yet less valuable. In the "Last Day" he hopes to illustrate the reassembly of the atoms that compose the human body at the "Trump of Doom" by the collection of bees into a swarm at the tinkling of a pan. The Prophet says of Tyre that "her merchants are princes." Young says of Tyre in his "Merchant,"

"Her merchants princes, and each DECK A THRONE."

Let burlesque try to go beyond him.

He has the trick of joining the turgid and familiar: to buy the alliance of Britain, "Climes were paid down." Antithesis is his favourite, "They for kindness hate:" and "because she's right, she's ever in the wrong." His versification is his own; neither his blank nor his rhyming lines have any resemblance to those of former writers; he picks up no hemistichs, he copies no favourite expressions; he seems to have laid up no stores of thought or diction, but to owe all to the fortuitous suggestions of the present moment. Yet I have reason to believe that, when once he had formed a new design, he then laboured it with very patient industry; and that he composed with great labour and frequent revisions. His verses are formed by no certain model; he is no more like himself in his different productions than he is like others. He seems never to have studied prosody, nor to have had any direction but from his own ear. But with all his defects, he was a man of genius and a poet.

MALLET.

Of David Mallet, having no written memorial, I am able to give no other account than such as is supplied by the unauthorised loquacity of common fame, and a very slight personal knowledge. He was by his original one of the Macgregors, a clan that became, about sixty years ago, under the conduct of Robin Roy, so formidable and so infamous for violence and robbery, that the name was annulled by a legal abolition; and when they were all to denominate themselves anew, the father, I suppose, of this author, called himself Malloch.

David Malloch was, by the penury of his parents, compelled to be Janitor of the High School at Edinburgh, a mean office of which he did not afterwards delight to hear. But he surmounted the disadvantages of his birth and fortune; for, when the Duke of Montrose applied to the College of Edinburgh for a tutor to educate his sons, Malloch was recommended; and I never heard that he dishonoured his credentials. When his pupils were sent to see the world, they were entrusted to his care; and having conducted them round the common circle of modish travels, he returned with them to London, where, by the influence of the family in which he resided, he naturally gained admission to many persons of the highest rank, and the highest character—to wits, nobles, and statesmen. Of his works, I know not whether I can trace the series. His first production was, "William and Margaret;" of which, though it contains nothing very striking or difficult, he has been envied the reputation; and plagiarism has been boldly charged, but never proved. Not long afterwards he published the "Excursion" (1728); a desultory and capricious view of such scenes of nature as his fancy led him, or his knowledge enabled him, to describe. It is not devoid of poetical spirit. Many of his images are striking, and many of the paragraphs are elegant. The cast of diction seems to be copied from Thomson, whose "Seasons" were then in their full blossom of reputation. He has Thomson's beauties and his faults. His poem on "Verbal Criticism" (1733) was written to pay court to Pope, on a subject which he either did not understand, or willingly misrepresented; and is little more than an improvement, or rather expansion, of a fragment which Pope printed in a miscellany long before he engrafted it into a regular poem. There is in this piece more pertness than wit, and more confidence than knowledge. The versification is tolerable, nor can criticism allow it a higher praise.

His first tragedy was Eurydice, acted at Drury Lane in 1731; of which I know not the reception nor the merit, but have heard it mentioned as a mean performance. He was not then too high to accept a prologue and epilogue from Aaron Hill, neither of which can be much commended. Having cleared his tongue from his native pronunciation so as to be no longer distinguished as a Scot, he seems inclined to disencumber himself from all adherences of his original, and took upon him to change his name from Scotch Malloch to English Mallet, without any imaginable reason of preference which the eye or ear can discover. What other proofs he gave of disrespect to his native country I know not; but it was remarked of him that he was the only Scot whom Scotchmen did not commend. About this time Pope, whom he visited familiarly, published his "Essay on Man," but concealed the author; and, when Mallet entered one day, Pope asked him slightly what there was new. Mallet told him that the newest piece was something called an "Essay on Man," which he had inspected idly, and seeing the utter inability of the author, who had neither skill in writing nor knowledge of the subject, had tossed it away. Pope, to punish his self-conceit, told him the secret.

A new edition of the works of Bacon being prepared (1740) for the press, Mallet was employed to prefix a Life, which he has written with elegance, perhaps with some affectation; but with so much more knowledge of history than of science, that, when he afterwards undertook the "Life of Marlborough," Warburton remarked that he might perhaps forget that Marlborough was a general, as he had forgotten that Bacon was a philosopher.

When the Prince of Wales was driven from the palace, and, setting himself at the head of the opposition, kept a separate court, he endeavoured to increase his popularity by the patronage of literature, and made Mallet his under–secretary, with a salary of two hundred pounds a year; Thomson likewise had a pension; and they were associated in the composition of The Masque of Alfred, which in its original state was played at Cliefden in 1740; it was afterwards almost wholly changed by Mallet, and brought upon the stage at Drury Lane in 1751, but with no great success. Mallet, in a familiar conversation with Garrick, discoursing of the diligence which he was then exerting upon the "Life of Marlborough," let him know that in the series of great men quickly to be exhibited he should FIND A NICHE for the hero of the theatre. Garrick professed to wonder by what artifice he could be introduced: but Mallet let him know that, by a dexterous anticipation, he should fix him in a conspicuous place. "Mr. Mallet," says Garrick, in his gratitude of exultation, "have you left off to write for the stage?" Mallet then confessed that he had a drama in his hands. Garrick promised to act it; and "Alfred" was produced.

The long retardation of the life of the Duke of Marlborough shows, with strong conviction, how little confidence can be placed on posthumous renown. When he died, it was soon determined that his story should be delivered to posterity; and the papers supposed to contain the necessary information were delivered to Lord Molesworth, who had been his favourite in Flanders. When Molesworth died, the same papers were transferred with the same design to Sir Richard Steele, who, in some of his exigencies, put them in pawn. They remained with the old duchess, who in her will assigned the task to Glover and Mallet, with a reward of a thousand pounds, and a prohibition to insert any verses. Glover rejected, I suppose, with disdain, the legacy, and devolved the whole work upon Mallet; who had from the late Duke of Marlborough a pension to promote his industry, and who talked of the discoveries which he had made; but left not, when he died, any historical labours behind him. While he was in the Prince's service he published Mustapha with a prologue by Thomson, not mean, but far inferior to that which he had received from Mallet for Agamemnon. The epilogue, said to be written by a friend, was composed in haste by Mallet, in the place of one promised, which was never given. This tragedy was dedicated to the Prince his master. It was acted at Drury Lane in 1739, and was well received, but was never revived. In 1740 he produced, as has been already mentioned, The Masque of Alfred, in conjunction with Thomson. For some time afterwards he lay at rest. After a long interval his next work was "Amyntor and Theodora" (1747), a long story in blank verse; in which it cannot be denied that there is copiousness and elegance of language, vigour of sentiment, and imagery well adapted to take possession of the fancy. But it is blank verse. This he sold to Vaillant for one hundred and twenty pounds. The first sale was not great, and it is now lost in forgetfulness.

Mallet, by address or accident, perhaps by his dependence on the Prince, found his way to Bolingbroke, a man whose pride and petulance made his kindness difficult to gain or keep, and whom Mallet was content to court by an act which I hope was unwillingly performed. When it was found that Pope clandestinely printed an unauthorised pamphlet called the "Patriot King," Bolingbroke in a fit of useless fury resolved to blast his memory, and employed Mallet (1749) as the executioner of his vengeance. Mallet had not virtue, or had not spirit, to refuse the office; and was rewarded, not long after, with the legacy of Lord Bolingbroke's works.

Many of the political pieces had been written during the opposition to Walpole, and given to Francklin, as he supposed, in perpetuity. These, among the rest, were claimed by the will. The question was referred to arbitrators; but, when they decided against Mallet, he refused to yield to the award; and, by the help of Millar the bookseller, published all that he could find, but with success very much below his expectation.

In 1775[sic], his masque of Britannia was acted at Drury Lane, and his tragedy of Elvira in 1763; in which year he was appointed keeper of the book of entries for ships in the port of London. In the beginning of the last war, when the nation was exasperated by ill success, he was employed to turn the public vengeance upon Byng, and wrote a letter of accusation under the character of a "Plain Man." The paper was with great industry circulated and dispersed; and he, for his seasonable intervention, had a considerable pension bestowed upon him, which he retained to his death. Towards the end of his life he went with his wife to France; but after a while, finding his health declining, he returned alone to England, and died in April, 1765. He was twice married, and by his first wife had several children. One daughter, who married an Italian of rank named Cilesia, wrote a tragedy called Almida, which was acted at Drury Lane. His second wife was the daughter of a nobleman's steward, who had a considerable fortune, which she took care to retain in her own hands. His stature was diminutive, but he was regularly formed; his appearance, till he grew corpulent, was agreeable, and he suffered it to want no recommendation that dress could give it. His conversation was elegant and easy. The rest of his character may, without injury to his memory, sink into silence. As a writer, he cannot be placed in any high class. There is no species of composition in which he was eminent. His dramas had their day, a short day, and are forgotten: his blank verse seems to my ear the echo of Thomson. His "Life of Bacon" is known, as it is appended to Bacon's volumes, but is no longer mentioned. His works are such as a writer, bustling in the world, showing himself in public, and emerging occasionally from time to time into notice, might keep alive by his personal influence; but which, conveying little information, and giving no great pleasure, must soon give way, as the succession of things produces new topics of conversation and other modes of amusement.

AKENSIDE.

Mark Akenside was born on the 9th of November, 1721, at Newcastle–upon–Tyne. His father Mark was a butcher, of the Presbyterian sect; his mother's name was Mary Lumsden. He received the first part of his education at the grammar–school of Newcastle; and was afterwards instructed by Mr. Wilson, who kept a private academy. At the age of eighteen he was sent to Edinburgh that he might qualify himself for the office of a dissenting minister, and received some assistance from the fund which the dissenters employ in educating young men of scanty fortune. But a wider view of the world opened other scenes, and prompted other hopes: he determined to study physic, and repaid that contribution, which being received for a different purpose, he justly thought it dishonourable to retain. Whether, when he resolved not to be a dissenting minister, he ceased to be a dissenter, I know not. He certainly retained an unnecessary and outrageous zeal for what he called and thought liberty; a zeal which sometimes disguises from the world, and not rarely from the mind which it possesses, an envious desire of plundering wealth or degrading greatness; and of which the immediate tendency is innovation and anarchy, an impetuous eagerness to subvert and confound, with very little care what shall be established.

Akenside was one of those poets who have felt very early the motions of genius, and one of those students who have very early stored their memories with sentiments and images. Many of his performances were produced in his youth; and his greatest work, "The Pleasures of Imagination," appeared in 1744. I have heard Dodsley, by whom it was published, relate that when the copy was offered him, the price demanded for it, which was a hundred and twenty pounds, being such as he was not inclined to give precipitately, he carried the work to Pope, who, having looked into it, advised him not to make a niggardly offer; for "this was no every–day writer."

Lives of the Poets

In 1741 he went to Leyden in pursuit of medical knowledge; and three years afterwards (May 16, 1744) became Doctor of Physic, having, according to the custom of the Dutch Universities, published a thesis or dissertation. The subject which he chose was "The Original and Growth of the Human Foetus;" in which he is said to have departed, with great judgment, from the opinion then established, and to have delivered that which has been since confirmed and received.

Akenside was a young man, warm with every notion that by nature or accident had been connected with the sound of liberty, and, by an eccentricity which such dispositions do not easily avoid, a lover of contradiction, and no friend to anything established. He adopted Shaftesbury's foolish assertion of the efficacy of ridicule for the discovery of truth. For this he was attacked by Warburton, and defended by Dyson; Warburton afterwards reprinted his remarks at the end of his dedication to the Freethinkers. The result of all the arguments which have been produced in a long and eager discussion of this idle question may easily be collected. If ridicule be applied to any position as the test of truth it will then become a question whether such ridicule be just; and this can only be decided by the application of truth, as the test of ridicule. Two men fearing, one a real, and the other a fancied danger, will be for a while equally exposed to the inevitable consequences of cowardice, contemptuous censure, and ludicrous representation; and the true state of both cases must be known before it can be decided whose terror is rational and whose is ridiculous; who is to be pitied, and who to be despised. Both are for a while equally exposed to laughter, but both are not therefore equally contemptible. In the revisal of his poem, though he died before he had finished it, he omitted the lines which had given occasion to Warburton's objections. He published, soon after his return from Leyden (1745), his first collection of odes; and was impelled by his rage of patriotism to write a very acrimonious epistle to Pulteney, whom he stigmatises, under the name of Curio, as the betrayer of his country. Being now to live by his profession, he first commenced physician at Northampton, where Dr. Stonehouse then practised, with such reputation and success, that a stranger was not likely to gain ground upon him. Akenside tried the contest a while; and, having deafened the place with clamours for liberty, removed to Hampstead, where he resided more than two years, and then fixed himself in London, the proper place for a man of accomplishments like his. At London he was known as a poet, but was still to make his way as a physician; and would perhaps have been reduced to great exigencies but that Mr. Dyson, with an ardour of friendship that has not many examples, allowed him three hundred pounds a year. Thus supported, he advanced gradually in medical reputation, but never attained any great extent of practice

112

or eminence of popularity. A physician in a great city seems to be the mere plaything of fortune; his degree of reputation is, for the most part, totally casual—they that employ him know not his excellence; they that reject him know not his deficience. By any acute observer who had looked on the transactions of the medical world for half a century a very curious book might be written on the "Fortune of Physicians."

Akenside appears not to have been wanting to his own success: he placed himself in view by all the common methods; he became a Fellow of the Royal Society; he obtained a degree at Cambridge; and was admitted into the College of Physicians; he wrote little poetry, but published from time to time medical essays and observations; he became physician to St. Thomas's Hospital; he read the Gulstonian Lectures in Anatomy; but began to give, for the Croonian Lecture, a history of the revival of learning, from which he soon desisted; and in conversation he very eagerly forced himself into notice by an ambitious ostentation of elegance and literature. His "Discourse on the Dysentery" (1764) was considered as a very conspicuous specimen of Latinity, which entitled him to the same height of place among the scholars as he possessed before among the wits; and he might perhaps have risen to a greater elevation of character but that his studies were ended with his life by a putrid fever June 23, 1770, in the forty–ninth year of his age.

Akenside is to be considered as a didactic and lyric poet. His great work is the "Pleasures of Imagination," a performance which, published as it was at the age of twenty–three, raised expectations that were not amply satisfied. It has undoubtedly a just claim to very particular notice as an example of great felicity of genius, and uncommon aptitude of acquisitions, of a young mind stored with images, and much exercised in combining and comparing them. With the philosophical or religious tenets of the author I have nothing to do; my business is with his poetry. The subject is well chosen, as it includes all images that can strike or please, and thus comprises every species of poetical delight. The only difficulty is in the choice of examples and illustrations; and it is not easy in such exuberance of matter to find the middle point between penury and satiety. The parts seem artificially disposed, with sufficient coherence, so as that they cannot change their places without injury to the general design. His images are displayed with such luxuriance of expression that they are hidden, like Butler's Moon, by a "Veil of Light;" they are forms fantastically lost under superfluity of dress. Pars minima est ipsa puella sui. The words are multiplied till the sense is hardly perceived; attention deserts the mind, and settles in the ear. The reader wanders through the gay diffusion, sometimes amazed, and sometimes delighted; but, after many turnings in the flowery labyrinth, comes out as he went in. He remarked little, and laid hold on nothing. To his versification justice requires that praise should not be denied. In the general fabrication of his lines he is perhaps superior to any other writer of blank verse; his flow is smooth, and his pauses are musical; but the concatenation of his verses is commonly too long continued, and the full close does not occur with sufficient frequency. The sense is carried on through a long intertexture of complicated clauses, and, as nothing is distinguished, nothing is remembered.

The exemption which blank verse affords from the necessity of closing the sense with the couplet betrays luxuriant and active minds into such self-indulgence that they pile image upon image, ornament upon ornament, and are not easily persuaded to close the sense at all. Blank verse will therefore, I fear, be too often found in description exuberant, in argument loquacious, and in narration tiresome. His diction is certainly poetical, as it is not prosaic; and elegant, as it is not vulgar. He is to be commended as having fewer artifices of disgust than most of his brethren of the blank song. He rarely either recalls old phrases, or twists his metre into harsh inversions. The sense, however, of his words is strained when "he views the Ganges from Alpine heights"—that is, from mountains like the Alps. And the pedant surely intrudes (but when was blank verse without pedantry?) when he tells how "Planets ABSOLVE the stated round of Time."

It is generally known to the readers of poetry that he intended to revise and augment this work, but died before he had completed his design. The reformed work as he left it, and the additions which he had made, are very properly retained in the late collection. He seems to have somewhat contracted his diffusion; but I know not whether he has gained in closeness what he has lost in splendour. In the additional book the "Tale of Solon" is too long. One great defect of this poem is very properly censured by Mr. Walker, unless it may be said in his defence that what he has omitted was not properly in his plan. "His picture of man is grand and beautiful, but unfinished. The immortality of the soul, which is the natural consequence of the appetites and powers she is invested with, is scarcely once hinted throughout the poem. This deficiency is amply supplied by the masterly pencil of Dr. Young, who, like a good philosopher, has invincibly proved the immortality of man from the grandeur of his conceptions and the meanness and misery of his state; for this reason a few passages are selected from the 'Night Thoughts,' which, with those from Akenside, seem to form a complete view of the powers, situation, and end of man."—"Exercises for Improvement in Elocution," p. 66.

His other poems are now to be considered; but a short consideration will despatch them. It is not easy to guess why he addicted himself so diligently to lyric poetry, having neither the ease and airiness of the lighter, nor the vehemence and elevation of the grander ode. When he lays his ill–fated hand upon his harp his former powers seem to desert him; he has no longer his luxuriance of expression or variety of images. His thoughts are cold, and his words inelegant. Yet such was his love of lyrics that, having written with great vigour and poignancy his "Epistle to Curio," he transformed it afterwards into an ode disgraceful only to its author.

Of his odes nothing favourable can be said; the sentiments commonly want force, nature, or novelty; the diction is sometimes harsh and uncouth, the stanzas ill–constructed and unpleasant, and the rhymes dissonant or unskilfully disposed, too distant from each other, or arranged with too little regard to established use, and therefore perplexing to the ear, which in a short composition has not time to grow familiar with an innovation. To examine such compositions singly cannot be required; they have doubtless brighter and darker parts; but, when they are once found to be generally dull, all further labour may be spared, for to what use can the work be criticised that will not be read?

GRAY.

Thomas Gray, the son of Mr. Philip Gray, a scrivener of London, was born in Cornhill, November 26, 1716. His grammatical education he received at Eton, under the care of Mr. Antrobus, his mother's brother, then assistant to Dr. George, and when he left school, in 1734, entered a pensioner at Peterhouse, in Cambridge. The transition from the school to the college is, to most young scholars, the time from which they date their years of manhood, liberty, and happiness; but Gray seems to have been very little delighted with academical gratifications; he liked at Cambridge neither the mode of life nor the fashion of study, and lived sullenly on to the time when his attendance on lectures was no longer required. As he intended to profess the common law, he took no degree. When he had been at Cambridge about five years, Mr. Horace Walpole, whose friendship he had gained at Eton, invited him to travel with him as his companion. They wandered through France into Italy; and Gray's "Letters" contain a very pleasing account of many parts of their journey. But unequal friendships are easily dissolved; at Florence they quarrelled and parted; and Mr. Walpole is now content to have it told that it was by his fault. If we look, however, without prejudice on the world, we shall find that men whose consciousness of their own merit sets them above the compliances of servility are apt enough in their association with superiors to watch their own dignity with troublesome and punctilious jealousy, and in the fervour of independence to exact that attention which they refuse to pay. Part they did, whatever was the quarrel; and the rest of their travels was doubtless more unpleasant to them both. Gray continued his journey in a manner suitable to his own little fortune, with only an occasional servant. He returned to England in September, 1741, and in about two months afterwards buried his father, who had, by an injudicious waste of money upon a new house, so much lessened his fortune that Gray thought himself too poor to study the law. He therefore retired to Cambridge, where he soon after became Bachelor of Civil Law, and where, without liking the place or its inhabitants, or professing to like them, he passed, except a short residence at London, the rest of his life. About this time he was deprived of Mr. West, the son of a chancellor of Ireland, a friend on whom he appears to have set a high value, and who deserved his esteem by the powers which he shows in his "Letters" and in the "Ode to May," which Mr. Mason has preserved, as well as by the sincerity with which, when Gray sent him part of Agrippina, a tragedy that he had just begun, he gave an opinion which probably intercepted the progress of the work, and which the judgment of every reader will confirm. It was certainly no loss to the English stage that Agrippina was never finished. In this year (1742) Gray seems to have applied himself seriously to poetry; for in this year were produced the "Ode to Spring," his "Prospect of Eton," and his "Ode to Adversity." He began likewise a Latin poem, "De Principiis Cogitandi."

It may be collected from the narrative of Mr. Mason that his first ambition was to have excelled in Latin poetry; perhaps it were reasonable to wish that he had prosecuted his design; for though there is at present some embarrassment in his phrase, and some harshness in his lyric numbers, his copiousness of language is such as very few possess; and his lines, even when imperfect, discover a writer whom practice would have made skilful. He now lived on at Peterhouse, very little solicitous what others did or thought, and cultivated his mind and enlarged his views without any other purpose than of improving and amusing himself, when Mr. Mason, being elected Fellow of Pembroke Hall, brought him a companion who was afterwards to be his editor, and whose fondness and fidelity has kindled in him a zeal of admiration which cannot be reasonably expected from the neutrality of a stranger and the coldness of a critic. In this retirement he wrote (1747) an ode on the "Death of Mr. Walpole's Cat;" and the year afterwards attempted a poem of more importance, on "Government and Education," of which the fragments which remain have many excellent lines. His next production (1750) was his far- famed

"Elegy in the Churchyard," which, finding its way into a magazine, first, I believe, made him known to the public.

An invitation from Lady Cobham about this time gave occasion to an odd composition called "A Long Story," which adds little to Gray's character. Several of his pieces were published (1753) with designs by Mr. Bentley; and, that they might in some form or other make a book, only one side of each leaf was printed. I believe the poems and the plates recommended each other so well that the whole impression was soon bought. This year he lost his mother. Some time afterwards (1756) some young men of the college, whose chambers were near his, diverted themselves with disturbing him by frequent and troublesome noises, and, as is said, by pranks yet more offensive and contemptuous. This insolence, having endured it awhile, he represented to the governors of the society, among whom perhaps he had no friends; and finding his complaint little regarded, removed himself to Pembroke Hall.

In 1759 he published "The Progress of Poetry" and "The Bard," two compositions at which the readers of poetry were at first content to gaze in mute amazement. Some that tried them confessed their inability to understand them, though Warburton said that they were understood as well as the works of Milton and Shakespeare, which it is the fashion to admire. Garrick wrote a few lines in their praise. Some hardy champions undertook to rescue them from neglect; and in a short time many were content to be shown beauties which they could not see.

Gray's reputation was now so high that, after the death of Cibber, he had the honour of refusing the laurel, which was then bestowed on Mr. Whitehead. His curiosity, not long after, drew him away from Cambridge to a lodging near the Museum, where he resided near three years, reading and transcribing, and, so far as can be discovered, very little affected by two odes on "Oblivion" and "Obscurity," in which his lyric performances were ridiculed with much contempt and much ingenuity. When the Professor of Modern History at Cambridge died, he was, as he says, "cockered and spirited up," till he asked it of Lord Bute, who sent him a civil refusal; and the place was given to Mr. Brocket, the tutor of Sir James Lowther. His constitution was weak, and, believing that his health was promoted by exercise and change of place, he undertook (1765) a journey into Scotland, of which his account, so far as it extends, is very curious and elegant; for, as his comprehension was ample, his curiosity extended to all the works of art, all the appearances of nature, and all the monuments of past events. He naturally contracted a friendship with Dr. Beattie, whom he found a poet, a philosopher, and a good man. The Mareschal College at Aberdeen offered him a degree of Doctor of Laws, which, having omitted to take it at Cambridge, he thought it decent to refuse. What he had formerly solicited in vain was at last given him without solicitation. The Professorship of History became again vacant, and he received (1768) an offer of it from the Duke of Grafton. He accepted, and retained, it to his death; always designing lectures, but never reading them; uneasy at his neglect of duty, and appeasing his uneasiness with designs of reformation, and with a resolution which he believed himself to have made of resigning the office if he found himself unable to discharge it. Ill–health made another journey necessary, and he visited (1769) Westmoreland and Cumberland. He that reads his epistolary narration wishes that, to travel, and to tell his travels, had been more of his employment; but it is by studying at home that we must obtain the ability of travelling with intelligence and improvement. His travels and his studies were now near their end. The gout, of which he had sustained many weak attacks, fell upon his stomach, and, yielding to no medicines, produced strong convulsions, which (July 30, 1771) terminated in death. His character I am willing to adopt, as Mr. Mason has done, from a letter written to my friend Mr. Boswell by the Rev. Mr. Temple, rector of St. Gluvias in Cornwall; and am as willing as his warmest well–wisher to believe it true:—

"Perhaps he was the most learned man in Europe. He was equally acquainted with the elegant and profound parts of science, and that not superficially, but thoroughly. He knew every branch of history, both natural and civil; had read all the original historians of England, France, and Italy; and was a great antiquarian. Criticism, metaphysics, morals, politics, made a principal part of his study; voyages and travels of all sorts were his favourite amusements; and he had a fine taste in painting, prints, architecture, and gardening. With such a fund of knowledge, his conversation must have been equally instructing and entertaining; but he was also a good man, a man of virtue and humanity. There is no character without some speck, some imperfection; and I think the greatest defect in his was an affectation in delicacy, or rather effeminacy, and a visible fastidiousness, or contempt and disdain of his inferiors in science. He also had, in some degree, that weakness which disgusted Voltaire so much in Mr. Congreve: though he seemed to value others chiefly according to the progress they had made in knowledge, yet he could not bear to be considered merely as a man of letters; and, though without birth or fortune or station, his desire was to be looked upon as a private independent gentleman, who read for his amusement. Perhaps it may be said, What signifies so much knowledge, when it produced so little? Is it worth taking so much pains to leave no memorial but a few poems? But let it be considered that Mr. Gray was to others at least innocently employed; to himself certainly beneficially. His time passed agreeably; he was every day making some new acquisition in science; his mind was enlarged, his heart softened, his virtue strengthened; the world and mankind were shown to him without a mask; and he was taught to consider everything as trifling and unworthy of the attention of a wise man except the pursuit of knowledge and practice of virtue in that state wherein God hath placed us."

To this character Mr. Mason has added a more particular account of Gray's skill in zoology. He has remarked that Gray's effeminacy was affected most "before those whom he did not wish to please;" and that he is unjustly charged with making knowledge his sole reason of preference, as he paid his esteem to none whom he did not likewise believe to be good.

What has occurred to me from the slight inspection of his letters in which my undertaking has engaged me is, that his mind had a large grasp; that his curiosity was unlimited, and his judgment cultivated; that he was a man likely to love much where he loved at all; but that he was fastidious and hard to please. His contempt, however, is often employed, where I hope it will be approved, upon scepticism and infidelity. His short account of Shaftesbury (author of the "Characteristics") I will insert:—

"You say you cannot conceive how Lord Shaftesbury came to be a philosopher in vogue; I will tell you: first, he was a lord; secondly, he was as vain as any of his readers; thirdly, men are very prone to believe what they do not understand; fourthly, they will believe anything at all, provided they are under no obligation to believe it; fifthly, they love to take a new road, even when that road leads nowhere; sixthly, he was reckoned a fine writer, and seems always to mean more than he said. Would you have any more reasons? An interval of about forty years has pretty well destroyed the charm. A dead lord ranks with commoners; vanity is no longer interested in the matter, for a new road has become an old one."

Mr. Mason has added, from his own knowledge, that though Gray was poor he was not eager of money, and that out of the little that he had he was very willing to help the necessitous. As a writer, he had this peculiarity—that he did not write his pieces first rudely, and then correct them, but laboured every line as it arose in the train of composition; and he had a notion, not very peculiar, that he could not write but at certain times, or at happy moments—a fantastic foppery to which my kindness for a man of learning and virtue wishes him to have been superior.

Gray's poetry is now to be considered; and I hope not to be looked on as an enemy to his name if I confess that I contemplate it with less pleasure than his Life. His ode "On Spring" has something poetical, both in the language and the thought; but the language is too luxuriant, and the thoughts have nothing new. There has of late arisen a practice of giving to adjectives derived from substantives the termination of participles; such as the CULTURED plain, the DAISIED bank; but I was sorry to see, in the lines of a scholar like Gray, the HONIED Spring. The morality is natural, but too stale; the conclusion is pretty.

The poem "On the Cat" was doubtless by its author considered as a trifle, but it is not a happy trifle. In the first stanza, "the azure flowers THAT blow" show resolutely a rhyme is sometimes made when it cannot easily be found. Selima, the cat, is called a nymph, with some violence both to language and sense; but there is no good use made of it when it is done; for of the two lines

"What female heart can gold despise?
What cat's averse to fish?"

the first relates merely to the nymph, and the second only to the cat. The sixth stanza contains a melancholy truth, that "a favourite has no friend;" but the last ends in a pointed sentence of no relation to the purpose. If WHAT GLISTERED had been GOLD, the cat would not have gone into the water; and if she had, would not less have been drowned.

"The Prospect of Eton College" suggests nothing to Gray which every beholder does not equally think and feel. His supplication to Father Thames to tell him who drives the hoop or tosses the ball is useless and puerile. Father Thames has no better means of knowing than himself. His epithet "buxom health" is not elegant; he seems not to understand the word. Gray thought his language more poetical as it was more remote from common use. Finding in Dryden "honey redolent of spring," an expression that reaches the utmost limits of our language, Gray drove it a little more beyond common apprehension by making "gales" to be "redolent of joy and youth."